The N

By Rev Andrew Murray
1897
Compiled by
RR
<u>Visit my Collection of Books</u>

Holy Land With RR
<u>http://www.HolyLandWithRR.com</u>
Learn Piano Hymns & Gospel Songs
<u>http://www.LearnPianoWithRosa.com</u>

From the Desk of Editor

I want to take this opportunity to thank you for buying my eBook.

If you had liked my eBook, please give me a feedback and drop me a review.

I have many other similar books like this one.

<u>Click here to visit my Collection of Books</u>

Connect with us in these 2 Websites & Facebook:

<u>Holy Land With RR Website</u>

<u>Learn to Play Piano & Gospel Hymns</u>

<u>Like Me in Facebook</u>

Write to us and we look forward to hear from you,

RR Publishing Company

The New Life
By Andrew Murray
© Copyright 2014
RR Classics
This Work is Originally Published in 1897 & now avaliable as public domain works.
RR Classics Publishing Company

4 *Andrew Murray*

Translator's Note

A glance at the pages of this little work will show that it is more elementary than the other writings of its honoured author. The reason is that is specially designed for young disciples who have but recently chosen the better part, and consequently need nothing so much as just to sit at the feet of Jesus and hear His word. Every minister of a congregation in which young people have been brought to the Lord, will remember the keen feeling of anxiety that swept over his heart as he contemplated their entrance on the duties and responsibilities of a public Christian confession. The supreme question at such a time is: How shall these young converts be built up in the knowledge of the truth? How shall they be best taught the real nature of the new life they have received, the dangers by which it is beset, and the directions in which its energy may safely go forth?

The desire to give a fitting answer to these questions has given rise to many excellent manuals. In connection with every time of revival, especially, new books for this circle of readers always make their appearance. As Mr. Murray indicates in the Preface, it was in the midst of such a happy period that the following chapters were written. The volume came under my notice whilst I was recently traveling in Holland. A brief inspection showed me that it was one of the most simple, comprehensive, and suggestive of its class. It is now translated into English from the latest Dutch edition, that the many thousands who have profited by Mr. Murray's other admirable works may have a suitable book to give or recommend to those who are setting their faces towards an earnest and fruitful Christian life.

That it will be very helpful to this end I cannot doubt: especially if the directions the author himself has given are faithfully adhered to. It will be noticed that the chapters are comparatively short; but every one of them has a considerable number of Biblical references. Let no reader be content to read what is written here without turning up and examining the texts marked. This practice, if persistently carried out, cannot fail to yield much recompense. There are just as many chapters in the book as Sabbaths in the year. What an additional blessing it would bring, if the members of a family who have had access to the book during the week, were to hear a chapter read aloud every Sabbath evening, and were encouraged to quote the texts in each that my have struck them most.

I have only to add that the volume is now translated and issued with Mr. Murray's cordial sanction. It has been to me a very pleasant task to put it into an English dress for my younger brethren throughout the country. Beyond this point, of course, my responsibility does not go. Should the book prove useful in guiding the feet of those who have come to the Lord yet further into the way of peace and holiness, it will be, both for author and translator, the answer to many a fervent prayer.

J.P.L.

Abbroath, September 1891

Preface

In intercourse with young converts, I have very frequently longed for a suitable book in which the most important truths that they have need of for the New Life should be briefly and simply set forth. I could not find anything that entirely corresponded to what I desired. During the services in which, since Whitsuntide 1884, I have been permitted to take part, and in which I have been enabled to speak with so many who professed to have found the Lord, and who were, nevertheless, still very weak in knowledge and faith, this want was felt by me still more keenly. In the course of my journey, I felt myself pressed to take the pen in hand. Under a vivid impression of the infirmities and the perverted thoughts concerning the New Life, with which, as was manifest to me from conversations I had with them, almost all young Christians have to wrestle, I wished, in some words of instruction and encouragement, to let them see what a glorious life of power and joy is prepared for them in their Lord Jesus, and how simple the way is to enjoy all this blessing.

I have confined myself in these reflections to some of the most important topics. The first is the Word of God as the glorious and sure guide, even for the simplest souls that will only surrender themselves to it. Then, as the chief element in the word, there is the Son, the gift of the Father, to do all for us. Thereupon follows what the Scriptures teach concerning Sin, as the only thing that we have to bring to Jesus, as that which we must give to Him, and from which He will set us free. Further, there is Faith, the great word in which is expressed our inability to bring or to do anything, and that teaches us that all our salvation must be received every day of our life as a gift from above. With the Holy Spirit also must the young Christian make acquaintance, as the Person through whom the word and Jesus, with all His work, and faith in Him, can become power and truth. Then there is the Holy Life of obedience and of fruitfulness, in which the Spirit teaches us to walk. It is to these six leading thoughts of the New Life that I have confined myself, with the ceaseless prayer that God may use what I have written to make His young children understand what a glorious and mighty life it is that they have received from their Father. It was often very unwillingly that I took leave of the young converts who had to go back to lonely places, where they could have little counsel or help, and seldom mingle in the preaching of the word. It is my sure and confident expectation that what the Lord has given me to write shall prove a blessing to many of these young confessors.

[I have, in some instances, attached the names of the places where the different portions of this manual were written; in others, the names of the towns where the substance of them was spoken, as a remembrance to the friends with whom I had intercourse.]

While writing this book I have had a second wish abiding with me. I have thought what I could possibly do to secure that my little book should not draw away attention from the word of God, but rather help to make the word more precious. I resolved to furnish the work with marginal references, so that, on every point that was treated of, the reader might be stirred up still to listen to the Word itself, to GOD HIMSELF.

I am hopeful that this arrangement will yield a double benefit. Many a one does not know, and had nobody to teach him, how to examine the Scriptures properly. This book may help him in his loneliness. If he will only meditate on one and another point, and then look up the texts that are quoted, he will get into the way of consulting God's word itself on that which he wishes to understand. But it may just as readily be of service in prayer meetings or social gatherings for the study of the word. Let each one read the portion fixed on at home and review those texts that seem to him the most important. Let the president of the meeting read the portion aloud once. Let him then request that each one who pleases should announce one and another text on that point which has struck him most.

We have found in my congregation that the benefit of such meetings for bringing and reading aloud texts on a point previously announced, is very great. This practice leads to the searching of God's word, as even preaching does not. It stirs up the members of the congregation, especially the young people, to independent dealing with the word. It leads to a more living fellowship amongst the members of Christ's body, and helps also their upbuilding in love. It prepares the way for a social recognition of the word as the living communication of the thoughts of God, which with Divine power shall work in us what is pleasing to God. I am persuaded that there is many a believing man and woman that asks what they can accomplish for the Lord, who along this pathway could become the channels of great blessing. Let them once a week bring together some of their neighbours or friends (sometimes two or three household live on one farm) to hear read out texts for which all have been previously searching: the Lord shall certainly give His blessing there.

With respect to the use of this book in retirement, I would fain request one thing more. I hope that no one will think it strange. Let every portion be read over at least three times. The great bane of all our converse with Divine things is superficiality. When we read anything and understand it somewhat, we think that this is enough. No: we must give time, that it may make an impression and wield its own influence upon us. Read every portion the first time with consideration, to understand the good that is in it, and then see if you receive benefit from the thoughts that are there expressed. Read it the second time to see if it is really in accordance with God's word: take some, if not all, of the texts that are adduced on each point, and ponder them in order to come under the full force of what God has said on the point. Let your God, through His word, teach you what you must think and believe concerning Him and His will. Read it then the third time to find out the corresponding places, not in the Bible, but in your own life, in order to know if your life has been in harmony with the New Life, and to direct your life for the future entirely according to God's word. I am fully persuaded that the time and pains spent on such converse with the word of God under the teaching of this or some book that helps you in dealing with it, will be rewarded tenfold.

I conclude with a cordial brotherly greeting to all with whom I have been permitted to mingle during the past year, in speaking about the precious Saviour and His glorious salvation: also to all in other congregations, who in this last season have learned to know the beloved Lord Jesus as their Redeemer. With a heart full of peace and love, I think of you all, and I pray that the Lord may confirm His work in you. I have not become weary of crying to you: the blessedness and the power of the New Life that is in you are greater than you know, are wonderfully great: only learn to know aright and trust in Jesus, the gift of God and the Scriptures, the word of God. Only give Him time to hold converse with you and to work in you, and your heart shall overflow with the blessedness of God.

Now to Him who is able to do more than exceedingly above all that we can ask or think, to Him be glory in the Church to all eternity.

Andrew Murray.
Wellington, 12th August 1885

1. The New Life

"For God so loved the world, that He gave His only begotten Son, that whosoever believeth in Him should not perish, but have eternal life."—John 3:16

"For ye died, and your life is hid with Christ in God. Christ is our life."—Col. 3:3,4

"We declare unto you the life, the eternal life, which was with the Father, and was manifested unto us. God gave unto us eternal life; and this life is in His Son. He that hath the Son hath the life." —1 John 1:2; 5:11-12

How glorious, then, is the blessing which every one receives that believes in the Lord Jesus. Not only does there come a change in his disposition and manner of life; he also receives from God out of heaven an entirely new life. He is born anew, born of God: he has passed from death into life. (John 1:12-13; 3:5,7; 5:24; 1 John 3:14; 5:1)

This new life is nothing less than Eternal Life. (John 3:15-16,36; 6:40,51; 5:25-26; Romans 6:11,23; 8:2; 1 John 5:12,13) This does not mean, as many suppose, that our life shall now no more die, but shall endure into eternity. No: eternal life is nothing else than the very life of God, the life that He has had in Himself from eternity, and that has been visibly revealed in Christ. This life is now the portion of every child of God. (1 John 1:3; 3:1, 5:11)

This life is a life of inconceivable power. Whenever God gives life to a young plant or animal, that life has in itself the power of growth, whereby the plant or animal as of itself becomes large. Life is power. In the new life, that is, in your heart, there is the power of eternity. (John 5:10,28; Heb. 7:16 ; 2 Cor 7:9; 8:4; Col. 3:3-4; Phil. 4:13) More certain than the healthful growth of any tree or animal is the growth and increase of the child of God, who in reality surrenders himself to the working of the new life.

What hinders this power and the reception of the new spiritual life is chiefly two things. The one is ignorance of its nature, its laws and workings. Man, even the Christian, has of himself not the least conception of the new life that comes from God: it surpasses all his thoughts. His own perverted thoughts of the way to serve and to please God, namely, by what he does and is, are so deeply rooted in him, that, although he thinks that he understands and receives God's word, he yet thinks humanly and carnally on Divine things. (Jos. 3:4; Matt. 16:23) Not only must God give salvation and life; He must also give the Spirit to make us know what He gives. Not only must He point out the land of Canaan, and the way thither; we must also, like the blind, be led every day by Himself. The young Christian must try to cherish a deep conviction of his ignorance concerning the new life, and of his inability to form right thoughts about it. This will bring him to the meekness and to the childlike spirit of docility, to which the Lord shall make His secret known. (Ps. 25:5,8-9; 143:8; Isa. 42:16; 64:4; Matt. 11:25; 1 Cor. 1:18-19; 2:7,10,12; Heb. 11:8)

There is a second hindrance in the way of faith. In the life of every plant and every animal and every child there lies sufficient power by which it can become big. In the new life, God has made the most glorious provision of a sufficient power whereby His child can grow and become all that he must be. Christ Himself is his life and his power of life. (Ps. 18:2; 27:1; 38:3; 34:8; John 14:19; Gal. 2:20; Col. 3:3,4) Yet, because this mighty life is not visible or cannot be felt, but works in the midst of human weakness, the young Christian often becomes of doubtful mind. He then fails to believe that he shall grow with Divine power and certainty. He does not understand that the believing life is a life of faith whereby he reckons on the life that is in Christ for him, although he neither sees, feels, nor experiences anything. (Hab. 2:4; Matt. 6:27; Rom. 1:17; Gal. 3:11; Heb. 10:38)

Let every one then that has received this new life, cultivate this great conviction: it is eternal life that works in me: it works with Divine power: I can and shall become what God will have me be: Christ Himself is my life: I have to receive Him every day as my life given by God to me, and He shall be my life in full power.

O my Father, who hast given me Thy Son that I may have life inHim, I thank Thee for the glorious new life that is now in me. Ipray Thee, teach me to know aright this new life. I willacknowledge my ignorance and the perverted thoughts which are in me,concerning Thy service. I will believe in the heavenly power of thenew life that is in me: I will believe that my Lord Jesus, whoHimself is my life, will by His Spirit teach me to know how I canwalk in that life. Amen.

Try now to apprehend and appropriate the following lessons in your heart;—

1. It is eternal life, the very life of God, that you have now received through faith.

2. This new life is in Christ, and the Holy Spirit is in you to bring over to you all that is in Christ. Christ lives in you through the Holy Spirit.

3. This life is a life of wonderful power. However weak you may feel, you must believe in the Divine power of the life that is in you.

4. This life has need of time to grow in you and to take possession of you. Give it time: it shall surely increase.

5. Forget not that all the laws and rules of this new life are in conflict with all human thoughts of the way to please God. Be very

much in dread of your thoughts, and let Christ, who is your life and
also your wisdom, teach you all things.

2. The Milk Of The Word

"As new-born babes, long for the spiritual milk that is without guile, that ye may grow thereby unto salvation"—1 Peter 2:2

Beloved young Christians, hear what your Father has to say in this word. You have just recently given yourselves to the Lord, and have believed that He has received you. You have thus received the new life from God. You are now as new-born infants: He would teach you in this word what is necessary that you may grow and wax strong.

The first point is: you must know that you are God's children. Hear how distinctly Peter says this to those just converted: (1 Pet. 1:23; 2:2,10,25) You have been born again,' you are new-born infants,' you are now converted,' you are now the people of God.' A Christian, however young and weak he is, must know that he is God's child. Then only can he have the courage to believe that he shall make progress, and the boldness to use the food of the children provided in the word. All Scripture teaches us that we must know and can know that we are children of God. (Rom 8:16; 1 Cor. 3:1,16; Gal. 4:6,7; 1 John 3:2,14,24; 4:13, 5:10,13) The assurance of faith is indispensable to a healthy powerful growth in the Lord. (Eph. 5:8; Col. 2:6; 1 Pet. 1:14,19)

The second point which this word teaches you is: you are still very weak, weak as new-bon children. The joy and the love which a young convert sometimes experiences do indeed make him think that he is very strong. He runs the risk of exalting himself, and of trusting in what he experiences. He must nevertheless learn much of how he must become strong in his Lord Jesus. Endeavour to feel deeply that you are still young and weak. (1 Cor. 3:1,13; Heb. 5:13,14) Out of this sense of weakness comes the humility which has nothing (Matt. 5:3; Rom 12:3,10; Eph. 4:2; Phil. 2:3,4; Col. 3:12) in itself, and therefore expects all from its Lord. (Matt. 8:8,15,27,28)

The third lesson is: the young Christian must not remain weak; he must grow and increase in grace; he must make progress and become strong. God lays it upon us as a command. His word gives us concerning this point the most glorious promises. It lies in the nature of the thing: a child of God must and can make progress. The new life is a life that is healthy and strong: when a disciple surrenders himself to it, the growth certainly comes. (Judg. 5:31; Ps. 84:8, 92:13,14; Prov. 4:18; Isa. 40:31; Eph. 4:14; 1 Thess. 4:1; 2 Pet. 3:18)

The fourth and principal lesson, the lesson which young disciples of Christ have most need of is: it is through the milk of the word that God's new-born infants can grow. The new life from the Spirit of God can be sustained only by the word from the mouth of God. Your life, my young brother, will largely depend on whether you learn to deal wisely and well with God's word, or whether you learn to use the word from the beginning as your milk. (Ps. 19:8,11; 119:97,100; Isa. 55: 2,3; 1 Cor. 12:11)

See what a charming parable the Lord has given us here in the mother's milk. Out of her own life does the mother yield food and life to her child. The feeding of the child is the work of the tenderest love, in which the child is pressed to the breast, and is held in the closest fellowship with the mother. And the milk is just what the weak child requires, food gentle and yet strong.

Even so is there in the word of God the very life and power of God. (John 6:63; 1 Thess. 2:13; Heb. 4:12) His tender love will through the word receive us into the gentlest and most intimate fellowship with Himself. (John 10:4) His love will give us out of the word what is, like warm soft milk, just fitted for our weakness. Let no one suppose that the word is too high or too hard for him. For the disciple who receives the word, and trustfully relies on Jesus to teach him by the Spirit, the word of God shall practically prove to be gentle sweet milk for new-born infants. (Ps 119:18; John 14:26; Eph. 1:17-18)

Dear young Christian, would you continue standing, would you become strong, would you always live for the Lord? Then hear this day the voice of your Father: As new-born babes, long for the spiritual milk that is without guile.' Receive this word into your heart and hold it fast as the voice of your Father: on your use of the word of God will your spiritual life depend. Let the word of God be precious to you above everything. (Ps 19:14,47,48,111,127)

Above all, forget not this: the word is the milk; the sucking or drinking on the part of the little child is the inner, living, blessed fellowship with the mother's love. Through the Holy Spirit your use of the milk of the word can become warm, living fellowship with the Living Love of your God. O long then very eagerly for the milk. Do not take the word as something that is hard and troublesome to understand: in that way you lose all delight in it. Receive it with trust in the love of the living God. With a tender motherly love will the Spirit of God teach and help you in your weakness. Believe always that the Spirit will make the word in you life and joy, a blessed fellowship with your God.

Precious Saviour, Thou hast taught me to believe Thy word, and Thouhast made me by that faith a child of God. Through that word, asthe milk of the new-born babes, wilt Thou also feed me. Lord, forthis milk shall I be very eager: every day will I long after it.Teach me, through the Holy Spirit and the word, to walk and holdconverse every day in living fellowship with the love of theFather. Teach me always to believe that the Spirit has been givenme with the word. Amen.

1. What texts do you consider the best for proving that the Scriptures teach us that we must know we are children of God?

2. What are the three points in which the sucking child is to us a type of the young child in Christ in his dealing with the word?

3. What must a young Christian do when he has little blessing in the reading of God's word? He must set himself through faith in fellowship with Jesus Himself: he must reckon that Jesus will teach him through the Spirit and so trustfully continue in the reading.

4. One verse chosen to meet our needs, read ten times and then laid up in the heart, is better than ten verses read once. Only so much of the word as I actually receive and inwardly appropriate for myself, is food for my soul.

5. Choose out for yourselves what you consider one of the most glorious promises about making progress and becoming strong; learn it by heart, and repeat it continually as the language of your positive expectation.

6. Have you learned well to understand what the great means for growth in grace is?

3. God's Word In Our Heart

"Therefore shall ye lay up these My words in your heart and in your soul."—Deut. 11:18

"Son of man, all My words that I shall speak unto thee, receive in heart."—Ezek. 3:10

"Thy word have I laid up in mine heart, that I might not sin against Thee."—Ps. 119:11

Long for the milk, that ye may grow thereby. This charming word taught every young Christian that, if he would grow, he must receive the word as milk, as the living participation of the life and the love of God. On this account is it of so great importance to know well how we must deal with the word. The Lord says that we must receive it and lay it in our heart. (Deut. 30:14; Ps. 1:2; 119:34,36; Is. 51:7; John 5:38; 8:31; 15:7; Rom. 10:8-9; Col. 3:16) The word must possess and fill the heart. What does that mean?

The heart is the temple of God. In the temple there was an outer court and an inner sanctuary. So also is it in the heart. The gate of the court is the understanding; what I do not understand cannot enter into the heart. Through the outer gate of the understanding, the word comes into the court. (Ps. 119:34; Mat.. 13:19; Acts 8:30) There it is kept by memory and reflection. (Ps. 119:15,16) Still it is not yet properly in the heart. From the court there is an entrance into the innermost sanctuary; the entrance of the door is faith. What I believe, that I receive into my heart. (John 5:38; Acts 8:37; Rom. 10:10,17) Here it then becomes held fast in love and in the surrender of the will. Where this takes place, there the heart becomes the sanctuary of God. His law is there, as in the ark, and the soul cries out: The law is within my heart.' (Ex. 25:16; Ps. 37:31; 40:9; Col. 3:16)

Young Christian, God has asked your heart, your love, your whole self. You have given yourself to Him. He has received you, and would have you and your heart entirely for Himself. He will make that heart full of His word. What is in the heart one holds dear, because one thinks continually on that which gives joy. God would have the word in the heart. Where His word is, there is He Himself and His might. He considers Himself bound to fulfill His word; when you have the word, you have God Himself to work in you. (Gen. 21:1; Josh. 23:14) He wills that you should receive and lay up His words in your heart: then will He greatly bless you. (Deut. 11:10; 28:1,2; Ps. 1:2,3; 119;14,45,98,165; John 27:6,8,17)

How I wish that I could bring all young Christians to receive simply that word of their Father, Lay up My words in your heart,' and to give their whole heart to become full of God's word. Resolve then to do this. Take pains to understand what you read. When you understand it, take then always one or another word to keep in remembrance and ponder. Learn words of God by heart; repeat them to yourself in the course of the day. The word is seed; the seed must have time, must be kept in the ground: so must the word be carried in the heart. Give the best powers of your heart, your love, your desire, the willing and joyful activity of your will, to God's word. Blessed is the man whose delight is in the law of the Lord; and in His law doth he meditate day and night.' Let the heart be a temple, not for the world and its thoughts, but for God and His thoughts. (Ps. 119:69; John 15:3,7; 17:6,8,17) He that, every day, faithfully opens his heart to God's voice to hear what God says, and keeps and carries about that word, shall see how faithfully God also shall open His heart to our voice, to hear what we say to Him in prayer.

Dear Christian, pray read yet once again the words at the head of this section. Receive them as God's word to you—the word of the Father who has received you as a child, of Jesus who has made you God's child. God asks of you, as His child, that you give your heart to become filled with His word. Will you do this? What say you? The Lord Jesus would complete His holy work in you with power along this way. (John 14:21,23; 1 John 2:14,24; Rev. 3:8,10) Let your answer be distinct and continuous: I have hid Thy word in my heart;' How love I thy law: it is my mediation all the day.' Even if it appears difficult for you to understand the word, read it only the more. The Father has promised to make it a blessing in your heart. But you must first take it into your heart. Believe then that God will by the Holy Spirit make it living and powerful in you.

O my Father, who hast said to me: My son, give Me thine heart,' Ihave given Thee mine heart. Now that Thou chargest me to lay up andto keep Thy word in that heart, I answer: I keep Thy commands withmy whole heart.' Father, teach me every day so to receive Thy wordin my heart that it can exercise there its blessed influence.Strengthen me in the deep conviction that even though I do notactually apprehend its meaning and power, I can still reckon on Theeto make the word living and powerful in me. Amen.

1. What is the difference between the reading of the word to increase knowledge and the receiving of it in faith?

2. The word is as a seed. Seed requires time ere it springs up. During this time it must be kept silently and constantly in the earth. I must not only read God's word, but ponder it and reflect upon it: then shall it work in me. The word must be in me the whole day, must abide in me, must dwell in me.

3. What are the reasons that the word of God sometimes has so little power in those that read it and really long for blessing? One of

the principal reasons is surely that they do not give the seed time to grow, that they do not keep it and reflect upon it, in the believing assurance that the word itself shall have its working.

4. What is the token of His disciples that Jesus mentions first in the high-priestly prayer? (John 17)

5. What are the blessings of a heart filled with the word of God?

4. Faith

"Blessed is she that believed; for there shall be a fulfilment of the things which have been spoken to her from the Lord."—Luke 1:45

"I believe God, that it shall be even so as it hath been spoken unto me.'—Acts 27:25

"Abraham waxed strong through faith, being fully assured that what He had promised, he was able also to perform."—Rom. 4:21

God has asked you to take and lay up His words in your heart. Faith is the proper avenue whereby the word is taken and received into the innermost depths of the heart. Let the young Christian then take pains always to understand better what faith is: he will thereby gain an insight into the reasons why such great things are bound up with faith. He will yield his perfect assent to the view that full salvation is made every day dependent on faith. (1 Chron. 22:20; Mk. 9:23; Heb. 11:33,35; 1 John 5:4,5)

Let me now ask my reader to read over once again the three texts which stand above, and to find out what is the principal thought that they teach about faith. Pray, read nothing actually beyond them, but read first these words of God, and ask yourself what they teach you about faith.

They make us see that faith always attaches itself to what God has said or promised. When an honourable man says anything, he also does it: on the back of the saying follows the doing. So also is it with God: when He would do anything, He says so first through

His word. When the man of God becomes possessed with this conviction and established in it, God always does for him what He has said. With God, speaking and doing always go together: the deed follows the word: Shall He say it and not do it?' (Gen. 21:1; 32:12; Num. 14:17,18,20; 23:19; Josh. 21:45; 23:14; 2 Sam. 7:25,29; 1 Kings 8:15,24; Ps. 119:49) When I have a word of God in which He promises to do something, I can always remain sure that He will do it. I have simply to take and hold fast the word, and there with wait upon God: God will take care that He fulfils His word to me. Before I ever feel or experience anything, I hold fast the promise, and I know by faith that God will make it good to me. (Luke 1:38,45; John 3:33; 4:50; 11:40; 20:29; Heb. 11:11,18)

What, now, is faith? Nothing other than the certitude that what God says is true. When God says that something subsists or is, then does faith rejoice, although it sees nothing of it. (Rom. 1:17; 4:5; 5:1; Gal. 3:27; Eph. 1:19; 3:17) When God says that He has given me something, that something in heaven is mine, I know by faith with entire certitude that it is mine. (John 3:16,17,36; 1 John 5:12,13) When God says that something shall come to pass, or that He will do something for me, this is for faith just as good as if I had seen it. (Rom. 8:38; Phil. 3:21; 1 Thess 5:24; 1 Pet. 1:4,5) Things that are, but that I have not seen, and things that are not yet, but shall come, are for faith entirely sure. Faith is the assurance of things hoped for, the proving of things not seen.' (Heb. 11:1) Faith always asks only for what God has said, and then relies on His faithfulness and power to fulfil His word.

Let us now review again the words of Scripture. Of Mary we read: Blessed is she that believed; for there shall be a fulfilment of the things which have been spoken to her from the Lord.' All things that have been spoken in the word shall be fulfilled for me: so I believe them.

Of Abraham it is reported that he was fully assured that that which had been promised, God was also able to fulfil. This is assurance of faith: to be assured that God will do what He has promised.

Exactly thus is it in the word of Paul: I believe God that it shall be even so as it hath been spoken unto me.' It stood fixed with him that God would do what He had spoken.

Young disciples in Christ, the new, the eternal life that is in you is a life of faith. And do you not see how simple and how blessed that life of faith is? I go every day to the word and hear there what God has said that He has done and will do. (Gal. 2:20; 3:2,5; 5:5,6; Heb. 10:35; 1 Pet. 1:2) I take time to lodge in my heart the word in which God says that, and I hold it fast, entirely assured that what God has promised, He is able to perform. And then in a childlike spirit I await the fulfilment of all the glorious promises of His word. And my soul experiences: Blessed is she that believed; for the things that have been spoken to her from the Lord shall be fulfilled. God promises—I believe—God fulfils: that is the secret of the new life.

O my Father, Thy child thanks Thee for this blessed life of faith inwhich we have to walk. I can do nothing, but Thou canst do all.All that Thou canst do hast Thou spoken in Thy word. And every wordthat I take and trustfully bring to Thee, Thou fulfillest. Father,in this life of faith, so simple, so glorious, will I walk withThee. Amen.

1. The Christian must read and search the Scriptures to increase his knowledge. For this purpose he daily reads one or more principal portions. But he reads the Scriptures also to strengthen his faith. And to this end he must take one or two verses to make them the subject of special reflection, and to appropriate them trustfully for himself.

2. Pray, do not suffer yourselves to be led astray by those who speak as if faith were something great and unintelligible. Faith is nothing other than the certitude that God speaks truth. Take some promises of God and say to Him: I know for certain that this

promise is truth, and that Thou wilt fulfil it. He will do it.

3. Never mourn over unbelief as if it were only a weakness which you cannot help. As God's child, however weak you may be, you have the power to believe, for the spirit of God is in you. You have only to keep in mind this: no one apprehends anything before that he has the power to believe; he must simply begin and continue with saying to the Lord that he is sure that His word is truth. He must hold fast the promise and rely upon God for the fulfilment.

5. The Power Of God's Word

Faith cometh of hearing, and hearing by the word of Christ.'—Rom. 10:17

Receive with meekness the implanted word, which is able to save your souls.'—James 1:21

We also thank God without ceasing, that, when ye received from us the word of the message, even the word of God, ye accepted it not as the word of men, but, as it is in truth, the word of God, which also worketh in you that believe.'—1 Thess. 2:13

For the word of God is living and active.'—Heb. 4:12

The new life of a child of God depends so much on the right use of God's word, that I shall once again speak of it with my young brothers and sisters in the Lord.

It is a great thing when the Christian discerns that he can receive and accomplish all only through faith. He has only to believe; God will look to the fulfilling of what is promised. He has every morning to trust in Jesus, and the new life as given in Jesus and working in himself; Jesus will see to it that the new life works in him.

But now he runs the risk of another error. He thinks that the faith that does such great things must be something great, and that he must have a great power in order to exercise such a great faith. (Luke 17:5-6; Rom. 10:6-8) And, because he does not feel this power, he thinks that he cannot believe as he ought. This error may prove a loss to him his life long.

Come and hear, then, how perverted this thought is. You must not bring this mighty faith to get the word fulfilled, but the word comes and brings you this faith which you must have. "The word is living and powerful." The word works faith in you. The Scripture says, "Faith is by the word." (Rom. 10:17; Heb. 4:12)

Think on what we have said of the heart as a temple, and of its two divisions. There is the outer court, with the understanding as its gate or entrance. There is the innermost sanctuary, with the faith of the heart as its entrance. There is a natural faith—the historic faith—which every man has; with this must I first receive the word into my keeping and consideration. I must say to myself, 'The word of God is certainly true. I can make a stand upon it.' Thus I bring the word into the outer court, and from within the heart desire reaches out to it, seeking to receive it into the heart. The word now exercises its divine power of life; it begins to grow and shoot out roots. As a seed which I place in the earth sends forth roots and presses still deeper into the soil, the word presses inwardly into the holy place. The word thus works true saving faith. (1 Thess. 2:13; Jas. 1:21; 1 Pet. 1:23)

Young Christian, pray understand this. The word is living and powerful; through the word you are born again. The word works faith in you; through the word comes faith. Receive the word simply with the thought that it will work in you. Keep yourselves occupied with the word, and give it time. The word has a divine life in itself; carry it in your inmost parts, and it will work life in you. It will work in you a faith strong and able for anything.

O be resolved then, pray, never to say, I cannot believe. You can believe. You have the Spirit of God in you. Even the natural man can say, This word of God is certainly true or certainly not true. And when he with a desire of the soul says, 'It is true; I will believe it,' the living Spirit, through whom the word is living and powerful, works this living faith. Besides, the Spirit is not only in the word, but also in you. Although you do not feel as if you were believing, know for certain you can believe. (Deut. 32:46,47; Josh. 1:7,9) Begin actually to receive the word; it will work a mighty faith in you. Rely upon it, that when you have to do with God's word, you have to do with a word that can be surely trusted that it of itself works faith in you.

And not only the promises, but also the commands have this living power. When I first receive a command from God, it is as if I felt no power to accomplish it. But if I then simply receive the word as God's word, which works in those that believe,—if I trust in the word to have its working, and in the living God which gives it its operation,—that commandment will work in me the desire and the power for obedience. When I weigh and hold fast the command, it works the desire and the will to obey; it urges me strongly towards the conviction that I can certainly do what my Father says. The word works both faith and obedience of faith. I must believe that through the Spirit I have the power to do what God wills, for in the word the power of God works in me. The word, as the command of the living God who loves me, is my power. (Rom. 1:3; 16:6; Gal. 6:6; 1 Thess. 1:3; Jas. 1:21)

Therefore, young disciples in Christ, learn to receive God's word trustfully. Although you do not at first understand it, continue to meditate upon it. It has a living power in it; it will glorify itself. Although you feel no power to believe or to obey, the word is living and powerful. Take it, and hold it fast; it will accomplish its work with divine power. The word rouses and strengthens for faith and obedience.

Lord God, I begin to conceive how Thou art in Thy word with Thy lifeand Thy power, and how that word itself works faith and obedience inthe heart that receives and keeps it. Lord, teach me to carry Thyevery word as a living seed in my heart, in the assurance that itshall work in me all Thy good pleasure. Amen

1. Forget not that it is one and the same to believe in the word, or in the person that speaks the word, or in the thing which is

promised in the word. The very same faith that receives the promises receives also the Father who promises, and the Son with the salvation which is given in the promises. Pray see to it that you never separate the word and the living God from each other.

2. See to it also that you apprehend thoroughly the distinction betwixt the reception of the word 'as the word of man' and 'as the word of God, which works in you that believe.'

3. I think that you now know what is necessary to become strong in faith. Exercise as much faith as you have. Take a promise of God. Say to yourself that it is certainly true. Go to God and say to Him that you rely on Him for the fulfilment. Ponder the promise, and cleave to it in converse with God. Rely upon Him to do for you what He says. He will surely do it.

4. The Spirit and the word always go together. I can be sure concerning all of which the word says that I must do it, that I also can do it through the Spirit. I must receive the word and also the command in the confidence that it is the living word of the living God which also works in us who believe.

6. God's Gift Of His Son

For God so loved the world, that He have His only-begotten Son, that whosoever believeth on Him should not perish, but have eternal life.'—John 3:16

Thanks be to God for His unspeakable gift.'—2 Cor. 9:15

Thus dear did God hold the world. How dear? That He gave His only-begotten Son for every one in the world who will trust in Him. And how did He give? He gave Him, in His birth as man, in order to be for ever one with us. He gave Him, in His death on the cross as Surety, in order to take our sin and curse upon Himself. He gave Him on the throne of heaven, in order to arrange for our welfare, as our Representative and Intercessor over all the powers of heaven. He gave Him in the outpouring of the Spirit, in order to dwell in us, to be entirely and altogether our own. (John 1:14,16; 14:23; Rom. 5:8; 8:32,34; Eph. 1:22; 3:17; Col. 2:9-10; Heb. 7:24,26; 1 John 4:9-10) Yes; that is the love of God, that He gave His Son to us, for us, in us.

Nothing less than His Son Himself. This is the love of God; not that He gives us something, but that He gives us some one—a living person—not one or another blessing, but Him in whom is all life and blessing—Jesus Himself. Not simply forgiveness, or revival, or sanctification, or glory does He give us; but Jesus, His own Son. The Lord Jesus is the beloved, the equal, the bosom-friend, the eternal blessedness of the Father. And it is the will of the Father that we should have Jesus as ours, even as He has Him. (Matt. 11:27; John 17:23,25; Rom. 8:38-39; Heb. 2:11) For this end He gave Him to us. The whole of salvation consists in this: to have, to possess, to enjoy Jesus. God has given His Son, given Him wholly to become ours. (Ps. 73:25; 142:6; John 20:28; Heb. 3:14)

What have we, then, to do? To take Him, to receive and to appropriate to ourselves the gift, to enjoy Jesus as our own. This is eternal life. He that hath the Son hath life.' (John 1:12; 2 Cor. 3:13,5; Col. 2:6; 1 John 5:12)

How I do wish, then, that all young Christians may understand this. The one great work of God's love for us is, He gives us His Son. In Him we have all. Hence the one great work of our heart must be to receive this Jesus who has been given to us, to consider Him and use Him as ours. I must begin every day anew with the thought, I have Jesus to do all for me. (John 15:5; Rom. 8:37; 1 Cor. 1:30; Eph. 1:3; 2:10; Phil. 4:13; 2 Tim. 1:12) In all weakness or darkness or danger, in the case of every desire or need, let your first thought always be, I have Jesus to make everything right for me, for God has given Him to me. Whether your need be forgiveness or consolation or confirmation, whether you have fallen, or are tempted to fall, into danger, whether you know not what the will of God is in one or another matter, or know that you have not the courage and the strength to do this will, let this always be your first thought, the Father has given me Jesus to care for me.

For this purpose, reckon upon this gift of God every day as yours. It has been presented to you in the word. Appropriate the Son in faith on the word. Take Him anew every day. Through faith you have the Son. (John 1:12; 1 John 5:9,13) The love of God has given the Son. Take Him, and hold Him fast in the love of your heart. (1 John 4:4,19) It is to bring life, eternal life, to you that God has given Jesus. Take Him up into your life; let heart and tongue and whole walk be under the might and guidance of Jesus. (2 Cor. 5:15; Phil. 3:8) Young Christian, so weak and so sinful, listen, pray, to that word. God has given you Jesus. He is yours. Taking is nothing else but the fruit of faith. The gift is for me. He will do all for you.

O my Lord Jesus, today anew, and every day, I take Thee. In all Thyfulness, in all Thy relations, without ceasing, I take Thee formyself. Thee, who art my Wisdom, my Light, my Leader, I take as myProphet. Thee, who dost perfectly reconcile me, and bring me nearto God, who dost purify and sanctify me and pray for me, I take asmy Priest. Thee, who dost guide and keep and bless me, I take as myKing. Thou, Lord, art All, and Thou art wholly mine. Thanks be toGod for His unspeakable gift. Amen.

1. Ponder much the word Give. God gives in a wonderful way: from the heart, completely for nothing, to the unworthy. And He gives effectually. What He gives He will really make entirely our possession, and inwardly appropriate for us. Believe this, and you shall have the certitude that Jesus will, to the full, come into your possession, with all that He brings.

2. Ponder much also that other word Take. To take Jesus, and to hold Him fast and use Him when received, is our great work. And that taking is nothing but trusting. He is mine with all that He has. Take Jesus—the full Jesus—every day as yours. This is the secret of the life of faith.

3. Then weigh well also the word Have. He that hath the Son hath light.' What I have is mine, for my use and service. I can dispose of it, and can have the full enjoyment of it. He that hath the Son hath life.'

4. Mark especially that what God gives, and what you take, and what you now have, is nothing less than the living Son of God.

Do you receive this?

7. Jesus' Surrender Of Himself

Christ also loved the Church, and gave Himself up for it; that He might sanctify it; that He might present the Church to Himself a glorious Church, not having spot or wrinkle; but that it should be holy and without blemish.'—Eph. 5:24-47

So great and wonderful was the work that Jesus had to do for the sinner, that nothing less was necessary than that He should give Himself to do that work. So great and wonderful was the love of Jesus towards us, that He actually gave Himself for us and to us. So great and wonderful is the surrender of Jesus, that all that same thing for which He gave Himself can actually and completely come to pass in us. For Jesus, the Holy, the Almighty, has taken it upon Himself to do it: He gave Himself for us. (Gal. 1:4; 2:20; Eph. 5:2,25; 1 Tim. 2:6; Titus 2:14) And now the one thing that is necessary is that we should rightly understand and firmly believe this His surrender for us.

To what end, then, was it that He gave Himself for the Church? Hear what God says. In order that He might sanctify it, in order that it might be without blemish. (Eph. 1:4; 5:27; Col. 1:22; 1 Thess. 2:10; 3:13; 5:23,24) This is the aim of Jesus. This His aim He will reach in the soul according as the soul falls in with it so as to make this also its highest portion, and then relies upon Jesus' surrender of Himself to do it.

Hear still a word of God: Who gave Himself for us, that He might redeem us from all iniquity, and purify unto Himself a people for His own possession, zealous of good works.' (Titus 2:14) Yes: it is to prepare for Himself a pure people, a people of His own, a zealous people, that Jesus gives Himself. When I receive Him, when I believe that He gave Himself to do this for me, I shall certainly experience it. I shall be purified through Him, shall be held fast as His possession, and be filled with zeal and joy to work for Him.

And mark, further, how the operation of this surrender of Himself will especially be that He shall then have us entirely for Himself: that He might present us to Himself.' that He might purify us to Himself, a people of His own.' The more I understand and contemplate Jesus' surrender of Himself for me, the more do I give myself again to Him. The surrender is a mutual one: the love comes from both sides. His giving of Himself makes such an impression on my heart, that my heart with the self-same love and joy becomes entirely His. Through giving Himself to me, He of Himself takes possession of me; He becomes mine and I His. I know that I have Jesus wholly for me, and that He has me wholly for Him. (Ex. 19:4,5; Deut. 26:17,18; Isa. 41:9,10; 1 Cor. 6:19,20; 1 Pet. 2:10)

And how come I then to the full enjoyment of this blessed life? I live in faith, the faith which is in the Son of God, who loved me and gave Himself up for me.' (John 6:29,35; 7:38; 10:10,38; Gal. 2:20) Through faith I reflect upon and contemplate His surrender to me as sure and glorious. Through faith I appropriate it. Through faith I trust in Jesus to confirm this surrender, to communicate Himself to me and reveal Himself within me. Through faith I await with certainty the full experience of salvation which arises from having Jesus as mine, to do all, all for me. Through faith, I live in this Jesus who loved me and gave Himself for me. and I say, No longer do I live, but Christ liveth in me.'

Christian, pray believe it with your whole heart: Jesus gives Himself for you: He is wholly yours: He will do all for you. (Matt. 8:10; 9:2,22; Mark 11:24; Luke 7:50; 8:48; 17:19; 18:42; Rom. 4:16,21; 5:2; 11:20; Gal. 3:25,26; Eph. 1:19; 3:17)

O my Lord Jesus, what wonderful grace is this, that Thou gavestThyself for me. In Thee is eternal life. Thou Thyself art the lifeand Thou givest Thyself to be in my life all that I need. Thoupurifiest me and sanctifiest me, and makest me zealous in goodworks. Thou takest me wholly for Thyself, and givest Thyself whollyfor me. Yes, my Lord, in all thou art my life. O make me rightlyunderstand this. Amen.

1. It was in His great love that the Father gave the Son. It was out of love that Jesus gave Himself. (Rom. 3:15; Eph. 5:26) The taking, the having of Jesus, is the entrance to a life in the love of God: this is the highest life. (John 14:21,23,; 17:23,26; Eph. 3:17,18) Through faith we must press into love, and dwell there. (1 John 4:16-18)

2. Do you think that you have now learned all the lesson, to begin every day with the childlike trust: I take Jesus this day to be my life, and to do all for me.

3. Understand that to take and to have Jesus, presupposes a personal dealing with Himself. To have pleasure in Him, to hold converse gladly with Him, to rejoice in Him as my friend and in His love—to this leads the faith that truly takes Him.

8. Children Of God

As many as received Him, to them gave He the right to become children of God, even to them that believe on His name.'—John 1:12

What is given must be received, otherwise it does not profit. If the first great deed of God's love is the gift of His Son, the first work of man must be to receive this Son. And if all the blessings of God's love come to us only in the ever-new, ever-living Son of the Father, all these blessings enter into us from day to day through the always-new, always-continuing reception of the Son.

What is necessary for this reception, you, beloved young Christians, know, for you have already received the Lord Jesus. But all that this reception involves must become clearer and stronger, the unceasing living action of your faith. (2 Cor. 10:15; 1 Thess. 1:8; 3:10; 2 Thess. 1:3) Herein especially consists the increase of faith. Your first receiving of Jesus rested on the certitude which the word gave you, that He was for you. Through the word must your soul be still further filled with the assurance that all that is in Him is literally and really for you, given by the Father in Him to be your life.

The impulse to your first receiving was found in your want and necessity. Through the Spirit you become still poorer in spirit, and you see everything every moment: this leads to a ceaseless, ever-active taking of Him as your all. (Matt. 5:3; 2 Cor. 3:10,13,16;

6:10; Eph. 4:14,15; Col. 2:6)

Your first receiving consisted in nothing but the appropriation by faith of what you could not yet see or feel. That same faith must be continually exercised in saying: all that I see in Jesus is for me: I take it as mine, although I do not yet experience it. The love of God is a communicating, a ceaseless outstreaming of His light of life over the soul, a very powerful and veritable giving of Jesus: our life is nothing but a continuous blessed apprehension and reception of Him. (John 1:16; Col. 2:9,10; 3:3)

And this is the way to live as children of God: as many as receive Him, to them gives He the power to become children of God. This holds true, not only of conversion and regeneration, but of every day of my life. If to walk in all things as a child of God, and to exhibit the image of my Father, is indispensable, I must take Jesus the only-begotten Son: it is He that makes me a child of God. To have Jesus Himself, to have the heart and life full of Him, is the way to live as a child of God. I go to the word and learn there all the characteristics of a child of God; (Matt. 5:9,16,44,45; Rom. 8:14; Eph. 1:4,5; 5:1,2; Phil. 2:15; Heb. 2:10; 1 Pet. 1:14,17; 1 John 3:1,10; 5:1,3) and after each one of them I write: this Jesus shall work in me: I have him to make me to be a child of God.

Beloved young Christian, learn, I beseech you, to understand the simplicity and the glory of being a true Christian. It is to receive Jesus, to receive Him in all His fulness, to receive Him in all the glorious relations in which the Father gives Him to you. Take Him as your Prophet, as your Wisdom, your Light, your Guide. Take Him as your Priest, who renews you, purifies you, sanctifies you, brings you near to God, takes you and forms you wholly for His service. Take Him as your King who governs you, protects you and blesses you. Take him as your Head, your Exemplar, your Brother, your Life, your All. The giving of God is a divine, an ever-progressive and effectual communication to your soul. Let your taking be the childlike, cheerful, continuous opening of mouth and heart for what God gives, the full Jesus and all His grace. To every prayer the answer of God is: Jesus, all is in Him, all in Him is for you. Let your response always be: Jesus, in Him I have all. You are, you live in all things as, children of God, through faith in Jesus Christ.'

O my Father, open the eyes of my heart to understand what it is tobe a child of God: to live always as a child through alwaysbelieving in Jesus, Thine only Son. O let every breath of my soulbe, faith in Jesus, a confidence in Him, a resting in Him, asurrender to Him, to work all in me.

If by the grace of God you now know that you have received Jesus and are God's child, you must now take pains to make His salvation known. There is many a one who longs to know and cannot find out how he can become a child of God.

Endeavour to make two things plain to him. First, that the new birth is something so high and holy that he can do nothing in it. He must receive eternal life from God through the Spirit: he must be born from above. This Jesus teaches. (John 3:1-8). Then make plain to him how low God has descended to us with this new life, and how near He brings it to us. In Jesus there is life for every one who believes in Him. This Jesus teaches (John 3:14-18). And this Jesus and the life are in the word. Tell the sinner that, when he takes the word, he then has Jesus, and life in the word. (Rom. 10:8). O do, pray, take pains to tell forth the glad tidings that we become children of God only through faith in Jesus.

9. Our Surrender To Jesus

They gave their own selves to the Lord.'— Cor. 8:5

In the surrender of Jesus for me, I have the chief element of what He has done and always does for me. In my surrender to Him I have the chief element of what He would have me to do. For young Christians who have given themselves to Jesus, it is a matter of great moment always to hold fast, to confirm and renew this surrender. This is the special life of faith, to say anew every day: I have given myself to Him, to follow Him and to serve Him; (Matt. 4:22; 10:24,25,37,38; Luke 18:22; John 12:25,26; 2 Cor. 5:15) He has taken me: I am His, and entirely at His service. (Matt. 28:20)

Young Christian, hold firm your surrender, and make it always firmer. When there recurs a stumbling or a sin after you have surrendered yourself, think not the surrender was not sincere. No; the surrender to Jesus does not make us perfect at once. You have sinned, because you were not thoroughly or firmly enough in His arms. Adhere to this, although it be with shame: Lord, Thou knowest it, I have given myself to Thee: I am Thine. (John 21:17; Gal. 6:1; 1 Thess. 5:24; 2 Tim. 2:13; 1 John 5:16) Confirm this surrender anew. Say to Him that you now begin to see better how complete the surrender to Him must be, and renew every day the voluntary, entire, and undivided offering up of yourselves to Him. (Luke 28:28; Phil. 3:7,8)

The longer we continue Christians, the deeper will be our insight into that word: surrender to Jesus. We shall always see more clearly that we do not yet fully understand or contemplate it. The surrender must become, especially, more undivided and trustful.The language which Ahab once used must be ours: According to thy saying, my lord, O king, I am thine, and all that I have' (1 Kings 20:4). This is the language of undivided dedication: I am thine, and all that I have. Keep nothing back. Keep back no single sin that you do not confess and leave off. Without conversion there can be no surrender. (Matt. 7:21,27; John 3:20,21; 2 Tim. 2:19,21) Keep back no single power. Let your head with all its thinking, your mouth with all its speaking, your heart with all its feeling, your hand with all its working—let your time, your name, your influence, your property, let all be laid upon the altar. (Rom. 6:13,22; 12:1; 2 Cor. 5:15; Heb. 8:15; 1 Pet. 2:5) Jesus has a right to all: He demands the whole. Give yourself, with all that you have, to be guided and used and kept, sanctified and blessed. According to Thy word, my Lord, O King, I am Thine, and all that I have.'

That is the language of trustful dedication. It is on the word of the Lord, which calls upon you to surrender yourself, that you have done this. That word is your warrant that He will take and guide and keep you. As surely as you give yourself, does He take you; and what He takes He can keep. Only, we must not take it again out of His hand. Let it remain fixed with you that your surrender is in the highest degree pleasing to Him: be certain of it, your offering is a sweet-smelling savour. Not on what you are, or what you experience or discover in yourselves, do you say this, but on His word. According to His word, you are able to take a stand on this: what you give, that He takes; and what He takes, that He keeps. (John 10:28; 2 Thess. 3:3; 2 Tim. 1:12) Therefore every day anew, let this be the childlike joyful activity of your life of faith: you surrender yourselves without ceasing to Jesus, and you are safe in the certitude that He in His love takes and holds you fast, and that His answer to your giving is the renewed and always deeper surrender of Himself to you.

According to Thy word, my Lord and King, I am Thine, and all that Ihave. Every day, this day, will I confirm it, that I am not mineown, but am my Lord's. Fervently do I beseech Thee to take fullpossession of Thy property, so that no one may doubt whose I am.Amen.

1. Ponder now once again the words giving and taking and having. What I give to Jesus, He take with a divine taking. And what He takes, he has and thereafter cares for. Now it is absolutely no longer mine. I must not take thought for it; I may not dispose of it. O pray, let your faith find expression in adoration: Jesus takes me: Jesus has me.

2. Should there overtake you a time of doubting or darkness whereby your assurance that the Lord has received you has come to be lost, suffer not yourself thereby to be dispirited. Come simply as a sinner, confess your sins: believe in His promises that He will by no means cast out those that come to Him and begin simply on the ground of the promises to say: I know that He has received me.

3. Forget not what the chief element in surrender is: it is a surrender to Jesus and to His love. Fix your eye, not upon your activity in surrender, but upon Jesus, who calls you, who takes you, who can do all for you. This it is that makes faith strong.

4. Faith is always a surrender. Faith is the eye for seeing the invisible. When I look at something, I surrender myself to the impression which it make upon me. Faith is the ear that hearkens to the voice of God. When I believe a message, I surrender myself to the influence, cheering or saddening, which the tidings exercises upon me. When I believe in Jesus, I surrender myself to Him, in reflection, in desire, in expectation, in order that He may be in me and do that for which He has been given to me by God.

10. Saviour From Sin

Thou shalt call His name Jesus; for it is He that shall save His people from their sins.'—Matt. 1:21

Ye know that He was manifested to take away sins; and in Him is no sin. Whosoever abideth in Him sinneth not.'—1 John 3:5,6

It is sin that is the cause of our misery. It is sin that provoked God, and brought His curse upon man. He hates sin with a perfect hatred, and will do everything to root it out. (Deut. 27:26; Isa. 59:1,2; Jer. 44:4; Rom. 1:18) It is to take away sin that God gave His Son, that Jesus gave Himself. (Gal. 2:4; Eph. 5:25,27; 1 Pet. 2:24; 1 John 3:8) It belongs to God to set us free, not only from punishment and curse, from disquietude and terror, but from sin itself. (Jer. 27:9; 1 Pet. 1:2,15,16; 2:14; 1 John 3:8) You know that He was manifested that He might take away our sins. Let us receive the thought deep into our hearts: it is for God to take away our sins from us. The better we apprehend this, the more blessed shall our life be.

All do not receive this. They seek chiefly to be freed from the consequences of sin, from fear and darkness, and the punishment that sin brings. (Gen. 27:34; Isa. 58:5,6; John 6:26; Jas. 4:3) Just on this account they do not come to the true rest of salvation. They do not understand that to save is to free from sin. Let us hold it fast. Jesus saves through taking away sin. Then we shall learn two things.

The first is to come to Jesus with every sin. (Ps. 32:5; Luke 7:38; 19:7,8,10; John 8:11; 34:36) the sin that still attacks and overmasters you, after that you have given yourself over to the Lord, must not make you lose heart. There must also be no endeavour merely in your own strength to take away and overcome sin. Bring every sin to Jesus. He has been ordained by God to take away sin. He has already brought it to nought upon the cross, and broken its power. (Heb. 9:26) It is His work, it is His desire to set you free from it. O learn then always to come to Jesus with every sin. Sin is your deadly foe: if you confess it to Jesus, and surrender it to Him, you shall certainly overcome it. (Rom. 7:4,9; 8:2; 2 Cor. 7:9; 2 Thess 2:3)

Learn to believe this firmly: this is the second point. Understand that Jesus, Jesus Himself, is the Saviour from sin. It is not you that must overcome sin with the help of Jesus, but Jesus Himself: Jesus in you. (Deut. 8:17,18; Ps. 44:4,8; John 16:33; 1 John 5:4,5) If you would thus become free from sin, if you would enjoy full salvation, let it be the one endeavour of your life to stand always in full fellowship with Jesus. Wait not till you enter into temptation ere you have recourse to Jesus. But let your life beforehand be always through Jesus. Let His nearness be your one desire; Jesus saves from sin; to have Jesus is salvation from sin (1 Cor. 15:10; Gal. 2:20; Phil. 4:13; Col 3:3-5) O that we could indeed rightly understand this! Jesus will not merely save from sin as a work that He will from time to time do in us, but He will give it as a blessing through Himself to us and in us. (Ex. 29:43; John 15:4,5; Rom. 8:10; Eph. 3:17,18) When Jesus fills me, when Jesus is all for me, sin has no hold on me: He that abideth in Him sinneth not.'

Yes: sin is driven out and kept out only through the presence of Jesus. It is Jesus, Jesus Himself, that, through His giving Himself to me and His living in me, is salvation from sin.

Precious Lord, let Thy light stream over me, and let it become stillclearer to my soul, that Thou, Thou Thyself, art my salvation.

Tohave Thee, Thee, with me, in me—this keeps sin out. Teach me tobring every sin to Thee; let every sin drive me into a closeralliance with Thee. Then shall Thy Jesus-name become truly mysalvation from sin. Amen.

1. See of what moment it is that the Christian should always grow in the knowledge of sin. The sin that I do not know, I cannot bring to Jesus. The sin that I do not bring to Him is not taken out of me.

2. To know sin better there are required:

The constant prayer, Examine me:' make known to me my transgression and my sin (Job 13:23; Ps. 139:23,24);

A tender conscience that is willing to be convinced of sin through the Spirit, as He also uses the conscience for this end;

The very humble surrender to the word, to think concerning sin only as God thinks.

3. The deeper knowledge of sin will be found in these results:

That we shall see to be sin things which previously we did not regard in this light;

That we shall perceive more the exceedingly sinful, the detestable character of sin (Rom. 7:13);

That with the overcoming of external sins we become all the more encouraged over the deep sinfulness of our nature, of the enmity of our flesh against God. Then we give up all hope of being or of doing anything good, and we are turned wholly to live in faith through the Spirit.

4. O let us thank God very heartily that Jesus is a Saviour from sin. The power that sin has had over us, Jesus now has. The place that sin has taken in the heart, Jesus will now take. The law of the Spirit of life in Christ Jesus has made us free from the law of sin and death.'

11. The Confession Of Sin

If we confess our sins, He is faithful and righteous to forgive us our sins, and to cleanse us from all unrighteousness.'—1 John 1:9

The one thing that God hates, that grieves Him, that He is provoked by, and that He will destroy, is sin. The one thing that makes man unhappy, is sin. (Gen. 6:5,6; Isa. 13:24; Ezek. 33:6; Rev. 6:16,17) The one thing for which Jesus had to give His blood was sin. In all the intercourse betwixt the sinner and God, this is thus the first thing that the sinner must bring to his God—sin. (Judg. 10:10,15,16; 2 Chron. 27:14; Ezra 9:6; Neh. 2:33; 9:2,33; Jer. 3:21,25; Dan. 9:4,5,20)

When you came to Jesus at first, you perceived this in some measure. But you should learn to understand this lesson more deeply. The one counsel concerning sin is, to bring it daily to the only One who can take it away—God Himself. You should learn that one of the greatest privileges of a child of God is—the confession of sin. It is only the holiness of God that can consume sin; through confession I must hand over my sin to God, lay it down in God, get quit of it to God, cast it into the fiery oven of God's holy love which burns against sin like a fire. God, yes, God Himself, and He alone, takes away sin. (Lev. 4:21; Num. 5:7; 2 Sam. 12:13: Ps. 32:5, 38:19; 51:5,19)

This the Christian does not always understand. He has an inborn tendency to desire to cover sin, or to make it less, or to root it out only when he purposes drawing near to God. He thinks to cover sin with his repentance and self-blame, with scorn of the temptation that came to him, or otherwise with what he has done or still hopes to do. (Gen. 3:12; Ex. 32:22,24; Isa. 1:11,15; Luke 13:26) Young Christian, if you would enjoy the gladness of a complete forgiveness and a divine cleansing of sin, see to it that you use aright the confession of sin. In the true confession of sin you have one of the most blessed privileges of a child of God, one of the deepest roots of a powerful spiritual life.

For this end, let your confession be a definite one. (Num 12:11, 21:7; 2 Sam. 24;10,17; Isa. 59:12,13; Luke 23:41; Acts 1:18,19; 22:19,20; 1 Tim. 1:13,15) The continued indeterminate confession of sin does more harm than good. It is much better to say to God that you have nothing to confess, than to confess you know not what. Begin with one sin. Let it come to a complete harmony betwixt God and you concerning this one sin. Let it be fixed with you that this sin is through confession placed in God's hands. you shall experience that in such confession there are both power and blessing.

Let the confession be an upright one. (Prov. 28:13; Lev. 26:40,41; Jer. 31:18,19) By it deliver up the sinful deed to be laid aside. By it deliver up the sinful feeling with a view to trusting in God. Confession implies renunciation, the putting off of sin. Give up sin to God, to forgive it to you, and to cleanse you from it. Do not confess, if you are not prepared, if you do not heartily desire to be freed from it. Confession has value only as it is a giving up of sin to God.

Let the confession be trustful (2 Sam. 12:13; Ps. 32:5; Isa. 4:7) Reckon firmly upon God actually to forgive you, and also to cleanse you from sin. Continue in confession, in casting the sin of which you desire to be rid into the fire of God's holiness until your soul has the firm confidence that God takes it on His own account to forgive and to cleanse away. It is this faith that really overcomes the world and sin: the faith that God in Jesus really emancipates from sin. (1 John 5:5; 2:12)

Brother, do you understand it now? What must you do with sin, with every sin? To bring it in confession to God, to give it to God; God alone takes away sin.

Lord God, what thanks shall I express for this unspeakable blessing,that I may come to Thee with sin. It is known to Thee, Lord, howsin before Thy holiness causes terror and flight. It is known toThee how it is our deepest thought, first to have sin covered, andthen to come to Thee with our desire and endeavour for good. Lord,teach me to come to Thee with sin, every sin, and in confession tolay it down before Thee and give it up to Thee. Amen.

1. What is the distinction betwixt the covering of sin by God and by man? How does man do it? How does God do it?

2. What are the great hindrances in the way of the confession of sin?

Ignorance about sin.

Fear to come with sin to the holy God.

The endeavour to come to God with something good.

Unbelief in the power of the blood and in the riches of grace.

3. Must I immediately confess an oath or a lie or a wrong word, or wait until my feeling has first cooled and become rightly disposed? O pray, confess it immediately; come in full sinfulness to God, without first desiring to make it less!

4. Is it also necessary or good to confess before man? It is indispensable, if our sin has been against man. And, besides, it is often good; it is often easier to acknowledge before God than before man that I have done something (Jas. 5:16).

12. The Forgiveness Of Sins

Blessed is he whose transgression is forgiven, whose sin is covered.'—Ps. 32:1

Bless the Lord, O my soul .... who forgiveth all thine iniquities.'—Ps. 103;2,3

In connection with surrender to the Lord, it was said that the first great blessing of the grace of God was this—the free, complete, everlasting forgiveness of all your sins. For the young Christian it is of great moment that he should stand fast in this forgiveness of his sins, and always carry the certitude of it about with him. To this end, he must especially consider the following truths.

The forgiveness of our sin is a complete forgiveness. (Ps. 103:12; Isa. 38:17; 55:7; Micah 7:18,19; Heb. 10:16-18) God does not forgive by halves. Even with man, we reckon a half forgiveness no true forgiveness. The love of God is so great, and the atonement in the blood of Jesus so complete and powerful, that God always forgives completely. Take time with God's word to come under the full impression that your guilt has been blotted out wholly and altogether. God thinks absolutely no more of your sins. I will forgive their iniquity, and their sin will I remember no more.' (Jer. 31:34; Heb. 8:12; 10:17)

The forgiveness of our sin restores us entirely again to the love of God. (Hos. 14:5; Luke 15:22; Acts 26:18; Rom. 5:1,5) Not only does God not impute sin any more,—that is but one half,—but He reckons to us the righteousness of Jesus also, so that for His sake we are as dear to God as He is. Not only is wrath turned away from us, but the fulness of love now rests upon us. I will love them freely, for Mine anger is turned away from him.' Forgiveness is access to all the love of God. On this account, forgiveness is also introduction to all the other blessings of redemption.

Live in the full assurance of forgiveness, and let the Spirit fill your heart with the certitude and the blessedness of it, and you shall have great confidence in expecting all from God. Learn from the word of God, through the Spirit, to know God aright, and to trust Him as the ever-forgiving God. That is His name and His glory. To one to whom much, yea, all is forgiven, He will also give much. He will give all. (Ps. 103:3; Isa. 12:1,3; Rom. 5:10; 8:32; Eph. 1:7; 3:5) Let it therefore be every day your joyful thanksgiving. Bless the Lord, O my soul, who forgiveth all mine iniquities.' Then forgiveness becomes the power of a new life: He who is forgiven much, loves much.' The forgiveness of sins, received anew in living faith every day, is a bond that binds anew to Jesus and His service. (John 13:14,15; Rom. 7:1; 1 Cor. 6:20; Eph. 5:25,26; Tit. 2:14; 1 Pet. 1:17,18)

Then the forgiveness of former sins always gives courage to go immediately anew with every new sin and trustfully to take forgiveness. (Ex. 34:6,7; Matt. 28:21; Luke 1:77,78) Look, however, to one thing: the certitude of forgiveness must not be a matter of memory or understanding, but the fruit of life—living converse with the forgiving Father, with Jesus in whom we have forgiveness. (Eph. 2:13,18; Phil. 3:9; Col. 1:21,22) It is not enough to know that I once received forgiveness: my life in the love of God, my living intercourse with Jesus by faith—this makes the forgiveness of sin again always new and powerful—the joy and the life of my soul.

Lord God, this is the wonder of Thy grace, that Thou art a forgivingGod. Teach me every day to know in this anew the glory of Thylove. Let the Holy Spirit every day seal forgiveness to me as ablessing, everlasting, ever-fresh, living, and powerful. And let mylife be as a song of thanksgiving. Bless the Lord, O my soul, whoforgiveth all thine iniquities.' Amen.

1. At bottom, forgiveness is one with justification. Forgiveness is the word that looks more to the relation of God as Father. Justification looks more to His acquittal as Judge. Forgiveness is a word that is more easily understood by the young Christian. But he must also endeavour to understand the word justification, and to obtain part in all that the Scripture teaches about it.

2. About justification we must understand—

That man in himself is wholly unrighteous.

That he cannot be justified by works, that is, pronounced righteous before the judgment-seat of God.

That Jesus Christ has brought in a righteousness in our place. His obedience is our righteousness.

That we through faith receive Him, are united with Him; and then are pronounced righteous before God.

That we through faith have the certitude of this, and, as justified, draw near before God.

That union with Jesus is a life by which we are not only pronounced righteous, but are really righteous and act righteously.

3. Let the certitude of your part in justification, in the full forgiveness of your sins, and in full restoration to the love of God, be every day your confidence in drawing near to God.

13. The Cleansing Of Sin

If we walk in the light, the blood of Jesus His Son cleanseth us from all sin. If we confess our sins, He is faithful and righteous to forgive us our sins, and to cleanse us from all unrighteousness.'—1 John 1:7,9

The same God that forgives sin also cleanses from it. Not less than forgiveness is cleansing a promise of God, and therefore a matter of faith. As it is indispensable, as it is impossible for man, so is cleansing as well as forgiveness certain to be obtained from God.

And what now is this cleansing? The word comes from the Old Testament. While forgiveness was a sentence of acquittal passed on the sinner, cleansing was something that happened to him and in him. Forgiveness came to him through the word: in the case of cleansing, something was done to him that he could experience. (Lev. 8:13; 14:7,8; Num. 19:12, 31:23,24; 2 Sam. 22:21,25; 2 Chron. 5:10; Neh. 13:30; 28:21,25; Ps. 21:4; Mal. 3:3) Consequently with us also cleansing is the inner revelation of the power of God whereby we are liberated from unrighteousness, from the pollution and the working of sin. Through cleansing we obtain the blessing of a pure heart; a heart in which the Spirit can complete His operations with a view to sanctifying us, and revealing God within us. (Ps 51:12; 73:1; Matt. 5:8; 1 Tim 1:5; 2 Tim. 2:22; 1 Pet. 1:22)

Cleansing is through the blood. Forgiveness and cleansing are both through the blood. The blood breaks the power that sin has in heaven to condemn us. The blood thereby also breaks the power of sin in the heart to hold us captive. The blood has a ceaseless operation in heaven from moment to moment. The blood has likewise a ceaseless operation in our heart, to purify, to keep pure the heart into which sin always seeks to penetrate from the flesh. The blood cleanses the conscience from dead works, to serve the living God. The marvelous power that the blood has in heaven, it has also in the heart. (John 13:10,11; Heb. 9:14; 10:22; 1 John 1:7)

Cleansing is also through the word, for the word testifies of the blood and of the power of God. (John 14:3) Hence also cleansing is through faith.It is a divine and effectual cleansing, but it must also be received in faith ere it can be experienced and felt. I believe that I am cleansed with a divine cleansing, even while I still perceive sin in the flesh; through faith in this blessing, cleansing itself shall be my daily experience.

Cleansing is ascribed sometimes to God or the Lord Jesus; sometimes to man. (Ps. 51:3; Ezek. 30:25; John 13:2; 2 Cor. 7:1; 1 Tim. 5:22; 2 Tim 2:21; Jas. 4:8; 1 John 3:3) That is because God cleanses us by making us active in our own cleansing. Through the blood the lust that leads to sin is mortified, the certitude of power against it is awakened, and the desire and the will are thus made alive. Happy is he that understands this. He is protected against useless endeavours after self-purification in his own strength, for he knows God alone can do it. He is protected against discouragement, for he knows God will certainly do it.

What we have now accordingly to lay the chief stress upon is found in two things, the desire and the reception of cleansing. The desire must be strong for a real purification. Forgiveness must be only the gateway or beginning of a holy life. I have several times remarked that the secret of progress in the service of God is a strong yearning to become free from every sin, a hunger and thirst after righteousness. (Ps. 19:13; Matt. 5:6) Blessed are such as thus yearn. They shall understand and receive the promise of a cleansing through God.

They learn also what it is to do this in faith. Through faith they know that an unseen, spiritual, heavenly, but very real cleansing through the blood is wrought in them by God Himself.

Beloved child of God, you remember how we have seen that it was to cleanse us that Jesus gave Himself. (Eph. 5:26; Tit. 2:14) Let Him, let God the Lord, cleanse you. Having these promises of a divine cleansing, cleanse yourselves. Believe that every sin, when it is forgiven you, is also cleansed away. It shall be to you according to your faith. Let your faith in God, in the word, in the blood, in your Jesus increase continually: God is faithful and righteous to cleanse us from all unrighteousness.'

Lord Go, I thank Thee for these promises. Thou givest not onlyforgiveness, but also cleansing. As surely as forgiveness comesfirst, does cleansing follow for every one that desires it andbelieves. Lord, let Thy word penetrate my heart, and let a divinecleansing from every sin that is forgiven me be the stableexpectation of my soul. Beloved Saviour, let the glorious,ceaseless cleansing of Thy blood through Thy Spirit in me be madeknown to me and shared by me every moment. Amen.

1. What is the connection between cleansing by God and cleansing by man himself?

2. What, according to 1 John 1:9, are the two things that must precede cleansing?

3. Is cleansing, as well as forgiveness, the work of God in us? If this is the case, of what inexpressible importance is it to trust God for it. To believe that God gives me a divine cleansing in the blood when He forgives me, is the way to become partaker of it.

4. What, according to Scripture, are the evidence of a pure heart?

5. What are clean hands'? (Ps. 24)

14. Holiness

Like as He which called you is holy, be ye yourselves also holy in all manner of living: because it is written, Ye shall be holy; for I am holy.'—1 Pet. 1:15,16

But of Him are ye in Christ Jesus, who was made unto us from God, sanctification.'—1 Cor. 1:30

God chose you from the beginning unto salvation in sanctification of the Spirit and belief of the truth.'—2 Thess. 2:13

Not only salvation, but holiness—salvation in holiness: for this end has God chosen and called us. Not only safe in Christ, but holy in Christ, must the goal of the young Christian be. Safety and salvation are in the long run found only in holiness. The Christian who thinks that his salvation consists merely in safety and not in holiness, will find himself deceived. Young Christian, listen to the word of God: Be holy.

And wherefore must I be holy? Because He who called you is holy, and summons you to fellowship and conformity with Himself. How should any one be saved in God, when he has not the same disposition as God? (Ex. 19:6; Lev. 11:44; 19:2; 20:6,7)

God's holiness is His highest glory. In His holiness His righteousness and love are united. His holiness is the flaming fire of His zeal against all that is sin, whereby He keeps Himself free from sin, and in love makes others also free from it. It is as the Holy One of Israel that He is the Redeemer, and that He dwells in the midst of His people. (Ex. 25:11; Isa. 2:6; 12:14; 43:15; 49:7; 57:15; Hos. 11:9) Redemption is given to bring us to Himself and to the fellowship of His holiness. We cannot possibly have part in the love and salvation of God if we are not holy as He is holy. (Isa. 10:18; Heb. 12:14) Young Christians, be holy.

And what is this holiness that I must have? Answer: Of God are ye in Christ, who of God is made unto you sanctification. Christ is your sanctification; the life of Christ in you is your holiness. (1 Cor. 1:3; Eph. 5:27) In Christ you are sanctified; you are holy. In Christ you must still be sanctified; the glory of Christ must penetrate your whole life.

Holiness is more than purity. In Scripture we see that cleansing precedes holiness. (2 Cor. 7:1; Eph. 5:26,27; 2 Tim. 2:21) Cleansing is the taking away of that which is wrong; liberation from sin. Holiness is the filling with that which is good, divine, with the disposition of Jesus. Conformity to Him—this is holiness: separation from the spirit of the world; the being filled with the presence of the Holy God—this is holiness. The tabernacle was holy because God dwelt there; we are holy, as God's temple, after we have the indwelling of God. Christ's life in us is our holiness. (Ex. 29:43,45; 1 Cor. 1:2; 3:16,17; 6:19)

And how do we become holy? By the sanctification of the Spirit. The Spirit of God is named the Holy Spirit, because He makes us holy. He reveals and glorifies Christ in us. Through Him Christ dwells in us, and His holy power works in us. Through this Holy Spirit the workings of the flesh are mortified, and God works in us both the will and the accomplishment. (Rom. 1:4; 8:2,13; 1 Pet. 1:2)

And what is now the work that we have to do to receive this holiness of Christ through the Holy Spirit? God chose you to salvation, in sanctification of the Spirit and belief of the truth.' (2 Thess. 2:13) The holiness of Christ becomes ours through faith. There must naturally first be the desire to become holy. We must cleanse ourselves from all pollutions of flesh and spirit by confessing them, giving them up to God, and having them cleansed away in the blood. Then, first, can we perfect holiness. (2 Cor. 7:1). Then, in belief of the truth that Christ Himself is our sanctification, we have to take and receive from Him what is prepared in His fulness for us. (John 1:14,16; 1 Cor. 2:9,10) We must be deeply convinced that Christ is wholly and alone our sanctification as He is our justification, and that He will actually and powerfully work in us that which is well-pleasing to God. In this faith we must know that we have sufficient power for holiness, and that our work is to receive this power from Him by faith every day. (Gal. 2:21; Eph. 2:10; Phil. 2:13; 4:13) He gives His Spirit, the Holy Spirit, in us; the Spirit communicates the holy life of Jesus to us.

Young Christian, the Three-One God is the Thrice-Holy. (Isa. 6:3; Rev. 4:8; 15:3,4) And this Three-One God is the God that sanctifies you: the Father, by giving Jesus to you, and confirming you in Jesus; the Son, by Himself becoming your sanctification and giving you the Spirit; the Spirit, by revealing the Son in you, preparing you as a temple for the indwelling of God, and making the Son dwell in you. O, be holy, for God is holy.

Lord God, the Holy One of Israel, what thanks shall I render toThess for the gift of Thy Son as my sanctification, and that I amsanctified in Him. And what thanks for the Spirit of sanctificationto dwell in me, and transplant the holiness of Jesus into me. Lord,give me to understand this aright, and to long for the experience ofit. Amen.

1. What is the distinction betwixt forgiveness and cleansing, and betwixt cleansing and holiness?

2. What made the temple a sanctuary? The indwelling of God. What makes us holy? Nothing less than this: the indwelling of God in Christ by the Holy Spirit. Obedience and purity are the way to holiness; holiness itself is something higher.

3. In Isa. 52:17, there is a description of the man who will become holy. It is he who, in poverty of spirit, acknowledges that, even when he is living as a righteous man, he has nothing, and looks to God to come and dwell in Him.

4. No one is holy but the Lord. You have as much of holiness as you have of God in you.

5. The word holy' is one of the deepest words in the Bible, the deepest mystery of the Godhead. Do you desire to understand something of it, and to obtain part in it? Then take these two thoughts, I am holy.' Be ye holy,' and carry them in your heart as a seed of God that has life.

6. What is the connection betwixt the perseverance of the saints and perseverance in holiness?

15. Righteousness

He hath showed thee, O man, what is good; and what doth the Lord require of thee, but to justly, and to love mercy, and to walk humbly with thy God?'—Micah 6:8

Present yourselves unto God, as alive from the dead, and your members as instruments of righteousness. Even so now present your members as servants to righteousness unto sanctification.'—Rom. 6:13,18,19

The word of Micah teaches us that the fruit of the salvation of God is seen chiefly in three things. The new life must be characterized, in my relation to God and His will, by righteousness and doing right; in my relation to my neighbour, by love and beneficence; in relation to myself, by humility and lowliness. For the present, we meditate on righteousness.

Scripture teaches us that no man is righteous before God, or has any righteousness that can stand before God; (Ps. 14:3; 143:2; Rom. 3:10,20) that man receives the rightness or righteousness of Christ for nothing; and that by this righteousness, which is received in faith, he is then justified before God, (Rom. 3:22,24: 10:3,10; 1 Cor. 1:30; 2 Cor. 5:21; Gal. 2:16; Phil. 3:9) he is right with God. This righteous sentence of God is something effectual, whereby the life of righteousness is implanted in man, and he learns to live as a righteous man, and to do righteousness. (Rom. 5:17,18; 6:13,18,19; 8:3; Tit. 1:8; 2:12; 1 John 2:29; 3:9,10) Being right with God is followed by doing right. The righteous shall live by faith' a righteous life.

It is to be feared that this is not always understood. One thinks sometimes more of justification than of righteousness in life and walk. To understand the will and the thoughts of God here, let us trace what Scripture teaches us on this point. We shall be persuaded that the man who is clothed with a divine righteousness before God must also walk before God and man in a divine righteousness.

Consider how, in the word, the servants of God are praised as righteous; (Gen. 6:9; 7:1; Matt. 1:19; Luke 1:6; 2:25; 2 Pet. 2:7) how the favour and blessing of God are pronounced upon the righteous; (Ps. 1:6; 5:13, 14:5; 34:16,20; 37:17,39; 92:13; 97:11; 144:8) how the righteous are called to confidence, to joy. (Ps. 32:11; 33:1; 58:11; 64:11; 68:4; 97:12) See this especially in the Book of Psalms. See how in Proverbs, although you should take but one chapter only, all blessing is pronounced upon the righteous. (Prov. 10:3,6,7,11,16,20,21,24,25,28,30,31,32 See how everywhere men are divided into two classes, the righteous and the godless. (Eccles 3:17; Isa. 3:10; Ezek. 3:18,20; 18:21,23; 33:12; Mal. 3:18; Matt. 5:45; 12:49; 25:46) See how, in the New Testament, the Lord Jesus demands this righteousness; (Matt. 5:6,20; 6:33) how Paul, who announces most the doctrine of justification by faith alone, insists that this is the aim of justification, to form righteous men, who do right. Rom. 3:31; 6:13,22; 7:4,6; 8:4; 2 Cor. 9:9,10; Phil 1:11; 1 Tim. 6:11) See how John names righteousness along with love as the two indispensable marks of the children of God. (1 John 2:4,11,29; 3:10; 5:2) When you put all these facts together, it must be very evident to you that a true Christian is a man who does righteousness in all things, even as God is righteous.

And what this righteousness is, Scripture will also teach you. It is a life in accordance with the commands of God, in all their breadth and height. The righteous man does what is right in the eyes of the Lord. (Ps. 119:166,168; Luke 1:6,75; 1 Thess. 2:10) He takes not the rules of human action; he asks not what man considers lawful. As a man who stands right with God, who walks uprightly with God, he dreads above all things even the least unrighteousness. He is afraid, above all, of being partial to himself, of doing any wrong to his neighbour for the sake of his own advantage. In great and little things alike, he takes the Scriptures as his measure and line. As the ally of God, he knows that the way of righteousness is the way of blessing, and life, and joy.

Consider, further, the promises of blessing and joy which God has for the righteous, and then live as one who, in friendship with God, and clothed with the righteousness of His Son through faith, has no alternative but to do righteousness.

O Lord, who hast said, There is no God else beside Me: a just Godand a Saviour,' Thou art my God. It is as a righteous God that Thouare my Saviour, and hast redeemed me in Thy Son. As a righteous GodThou makest me also righteous, and sayest to me that the righteousshall live by faith. O Lord, let the new life in me be the life offaith, the life of a righteous man. Amen.

1. Observe the connection between the doing of righteousness and sanctification in Rom. 6:19,22; Present your members as servants to righteousness unto sanctification.' Having become servants to God, ye have your fruit unto sanctification.' The doing of righteousness, righteousness in conduct and action, is the way to holiness. Obedience is the way to become filled with the Holy Ghost. And the indwelling of God through the Spirit—this is holiness.

2. Suffer it now: for thus it becometh us to fulfil all righteousness. It was when the Lord Jesus had spoken that word that He was baptized with the Spirit. Let us set aside every temptation not to walk in full obedience towards God, even as He did, and we too shall be filled with the Spirit. Blessed are they that hunger and thirst after righteousness.'

3. Take pains to set before yourselves the image of a man who so walks that the name of righteous; is involuntarily given to him. Think of his uprightness, his conscientious care to cause no one to suffer the least injury, his holy fear and carefulness to transgress none of the commands of the Lord—righteous, and walking in all the commandments and ordinances of the Lord blameless; and then say to the Lord that you should so live.

4. You understand now the great word, The righteous shall live by faith.' By faith the godless is justified, and becomes a righteous man; by faith he lives as a righteous man.

16. Love

A new commandment I give unto you, That ye love one another; even as I have loved you, that ye also love one another. By this shall all men know that ye are My disciples, if ye have love one to another.'—John 13:34,35

Love worketh no ill to his neighbour: love therefore is the fulfilling of the law.'—Rom. 13:10

Beloved, if God so loved us, we also ought to love one another. If we love one another, God abideth in us, and His love is perfected in us.'—1 John 4:11,12

In the word of Micah, in the previous section, righteousness was the first thing, to love mercy the second, that God demands. Righteousness stood more in the foreground in the Old Testament: it is in the New Testament that it is first seen that love is supreme. Utterances to this effect are not difficult to find. It is in the advent of Jesus that the love of God is first revealed; that the new, the eternal life, is first given; that we become children of the Father, and brethren of one another. On this ground the Lord can then, for the first time, speak of the New Commandment—the commandment of brotherly love. Righteousness is required not less in the New Testament than in the Old. (Matt 5:6,17,20; 6:33) Yet the burden of the New Testament is, that power has been given us for a love that in early days was impossible. (Rom. 5:5; Gal. 5:22; 1 Thess. 4:9; 1 John 4:11; 13:34)

Let every Christian take it deeply to heart, that in the first and the great commandment, the new commandment given by Jesus at His departure, the peculiar characteristic of a disciple of Jesus is brotherly love. And let him with his whole heart yield himself to Him, to obey that command. For the right exercise of this brotherly love, one must take heed to more than one thing.

Love to the brethren arises from the love of the Father. By the Holy Spirit, the love of God is shed abroad in our hearts, the wonderful love of the Father is unveiled to us, so that His love becomes the life and the joy of our soul. Out of this fountain of the love of God to us springs our love to Him. (Rom. 5:5; 1 John 4:19) And our love to Him works naturally love to the brethren. (Eph. 4:2,6; 5:1,2; 1 John 3:1; 4:7,20; 5:1) Do not attempt then to fulfil the commandment of brotherly love of yourselves: you are not in a position to do this. But believe that the Holy Spirit, who is in you to make known the love of God to you, also certainly enables you to yield this love. Never say: I feel no love; I do not feel as if I can forgive this man. Feeling is not the rule of your duty, but the command, and the faith that God gives power to obey the command. In obedience to the Father, with the choice of your will, and in faith that the Holy Spirit gives you power, begin to say: I will love him; I do love him. The feeling will follow the faith. Grace gives power for all that the Father asks of you. (Matt. 5:44,45; Gal 2:20; 1 Thess. 3:12,13; 5:24; Phil. 4:13; 1 Pet. 1:22)

Brotherly love has its measure and rule in the love of Jesus. This is my commandment, that ye love one another, as I have loved you.' (Luke 22:26,27; John 13:14,15,34; Col. 2:13) The eternal life that works in us is the life of Jesus; it knows no other law than what we see in Him; it works with power in us what it wrought in Him. Jesus Himself lives in us and loves in and through us: we must believe in the power of this love in us, and in that faith love as He loved. O, do believe that this is true salvation, to love even as Jesus loves.

Brotherly love must be in deed and in truth. (Matt. 12:50; 25:40; Rom. 13:10; 1 Cor. 7:19; Gal. 5:6; Jas. 2:15,16; 1 John 3:16-18) It is not mere feeling: faith working by love is what has power in Christ. It manifests itself in all the dispositions that are enumerated in the word of God. Contemplate its glorious image in 1 Cor. 13:4-7. Mark all the glorious encouragements to gentleness, to longsuffering, to mercy. (Gal. 5:22; Eph. 4:2,32; Phil. 2:2,3; Col. 3:12; 2 Thess. 1:3) In all your conduct, let it be seen that the love of Christ dwells in you. Let your love be a helpful, self-sacrificing love, like that of Jesus. Hold all children of God, however sinful or perverse they may be, fervently dear. Let love to them teach you to love all men. (Luke 6:32,35; 1 Pet. 1:22; 2 Pet. 1:7) Let your household, and the Church, and the world, see in you one with whom love is greatest;' one in whom the love of God has a full dwelling, a free working.

Christian, God is love. Jesus is the gift of this love, to bring love to you, to transplant you into that life of godlike love. Live in that faith, and you shall not complain that you have no power to love: the love of the Spirit shall be your power and your life.

Beloved Saviour, I discern more clearly that the whole of the newlife is a life in love. Thou Thyself art the Son of God's love, thegift of His love, come to introduce us into His love, and give us adwelling there. And the Holy Spirit is given to shed abroad thelove of God in our hearts, to open a spring out of which shallstream love to Thee, and to the brethren, and to all mankind. Lord,here am I, one redeemed by love, to love for it, and in its might tolove all. Amen.

1. Those who reject the word of God sometimes say that it is of no moment what we believe, if we but have love, and so they are for making love the one condition of salvation. In their zeal against this view, the orthodox party have sometimes presented faith in justification, as if love were not of so much importance. This is likely to be very dangerous. God is love. His Son is the gift, the

bringer, of His love to us. The Spirit sheds abroad the love of God in the heart. The New Life is a life in love. Love is the greatest thing. Let it be the chief element in our life: true love, that, namely, which is known in the keeping of God's commandments. (See 1 John 3:10,23,24; 5:2)

2. Do not wonder that I have said to you that you must love, although you do not feel the least love. Not the feeling, but the will is your power: it is not in your feeling, but in faith, that the Spirit in you is the power of your will to work in you all that the Father bids you. Therefore, although you feel absolutely no love to your enemy, say in the obedience of faith: Father, I love him; in faith in the hidden working of the Spirit in my heart, I do love him.

3. Pray, think not that this is love, if you wish no evil to any one, or if you should be willing to help, if he were in need. No: love is much more: love is love. Love is the disposition with which God addressed you when you were His enemy, and afterwards ran to you with tender longing to bless you.

17. Humility

And what doth the Lord require of thee, but to do justly, and to love mercy, and to walk humbly with thy God?'—Micah 6:8

Learn of me that I am meek and lowly in heart: and ye shall find rest unto your souls.'—Matt. 11:29

One of the most dangerous enemies against which the young Christian must watch, is pride or self-exaltation. There is no sin that works more cunningly and more hiddenly. It knows how to penetrate into everything, even into our service for God, our prayers—yea, even into our humility: there is nothing so small in the earthly life, nothing so holy in the spiritual life, that self-exaltation does not know to extract its nutriment out of. (2 Chron. 26:5,16; 32:26,31; Isa. 65:5; Jer. 7:4; 2 Cor. 12:7) The Christian must therefore be on his guard against it, must listen to what Scripture teaches about it, and about the lowliness whereby it is driven out.

Man was created to have part in the glory of God. He obtains this by surrendering himself to the glorification of God. The more he seeks that the glory of God only shall be seen in him, the more does this glory rest upon himself. (Isa. 43:7,21; John 12:28; 13:31,32; 27:1,4,5; 1 Cor. 10:31; 2 Thess. 1:11,12) The more he forgets and loses himself, desiring to be nothing, that God may be all and be alone glorified, the more happy shall he be.

By sin this design has been thwarted: man seeks himself and his own will. (Rom. 1:21,23) Grace has come to restore what sin has corrupted, and to bring man to glory by the pathway of dying unto himself and living solely for the glory of God. This is the humility or lowliness of which Jesus is the exemplar: He took no thought for Himself, He have himself over wholly to glorify the Father (John 8:50 Phil. 2:7)

He who would be freed from self-exaltation must not think to obtain this by striving against its mere workings. No: pride must be driven out and kept out by humility. The Spirit of life in Christ, the Spirit of His lowliness, will work in us true lowliness. (Rom. 8:2; Phil. 2:5)

The means that He will chiefly use for this end is the word. It is by the word that we are cleansed from sin; it is by the word that we are sanctified and filled with the love of God.

Observe what the word says about this point. It speaks of God's aversion to pride, and the punishment that comes upon it. (Ps. 31:24; Prov. 26:5; Matt. 23:12; Luke 1:51; Jas. 4:5; 1 Pet. 5:5) It gives the most glorious promises to the lowly. (Ps. 34:19; Prov. 11:2; Isa. 57: 15; Luke 9:48; 14:11; 18:14) In well-nigh every Epistle, humility is commended to Christians as one of the first virtues. (Rom. 12:3,16; 1 Cor. 13:4; Gal. 5:22,26; Eph. 4:2; Phil. 2:3; Col. 2:13) It is the feature in the image of Jesus which He seeks chiefly to impress on His disciples. His whole incarnation and redemption has its roots in His humiliation. (Matt. 20:26,28; Luke 22:27; John 13:14,15; Phil. 2:7,8)

Take singly some of these words of God from time to time and lay them up in your heart. The tree of life yields many different kinds of seed—the seed also of the heavenly plant, lowliness. The seeds are the words of God. Carry them in your heart: they shall shoot up and yield fruit. (1 Thess. 2:13; Heb. 4:12; Jas. 1:21)

Consider, moreover, how lovely, how becoming, how well-pleasing to God, lowliness is. As man, created for the honour

of God, you find it befitting you. (Gen. 1:27; 1 Cor. 11:7) As a
sinner, deeply unworthy, you have nothing more to urge against it.
(Job 40:6; Isa. 6:5; Luke 5:8) As a redeemed soul, who knows that
only through the death of the natural I does the way to the new life
lie, you find it indispensable. (Rom. 7:18; 1 Cor. 25:9,10; Gal.
2:20)

But here, as everywhere in the life of grace, let faith be the chief
thing. Believe in the power of the eternal life that works in you.
Believe in the power of Jesus, who is your life. Believe in the power
of the Holy Spirit who dwells in you. Attempt not to hide your
pride, or to forget it, or to root it out yourself. Confess this sin,
with every working of it that you trace, in the sure confidence that
the blood cleanses, that the Spirit sanctifies. Learn of Jesus that He
is meek and lowly in heart. Consider that He is your life, with all
that He has. Believe that He gives His humility to you. The word:
Do it to the Lord Jesus,' means, Be clothed with the Lord Jesus.' Be
clothed with humility, in order that you may be clothed with Jesus.
It is Christ in you that shall fill you with humility.

Blessed Lord Jesus, there never was any one amongst the
children ofmen so high, so holy, so glorious as Thou. And never
was there anyone who was so lowly and ready to deny himself as the
servant ofall. O Lord, when shall we learn that lowliness is the
grace bywhich man can be most closely conformed to the divine
glory? Oteach me this. Amen.

1. Take heed that you do nothing to feed pride on the part of
others. Take heed that you do not suffer others to feed your pride.
Take heed, above all, that you do nothing yourself to feed your
pride. Let God alone always and in all things obtain the honour.
Endeavour to observe all that is good in His children, and to thank
Him heartily for it. Thank Him for all that helps you to hold
yourself in small esteem, whether it be sent through friend or foe.
Resolve, especially, never on any account to be eagerly bent on your
own honour, when this is not accorded to you as it ought to be.

Commit this to the Father: take heed only to His honour.

2. By no means suppose that faint-heartedness or doubting is lowliness. Deep humility and strong faith go together. The centurion who said: I am not worthy that Thou shouldst come under my roof,' and the woman who said: Yea, Lord, yet even the dogs eat of the crumbs'—these two were the most humble and the most trustful that the Lord found (see Matt. 8:10; 15:28). The reason is this: the nearer we are to God, the less we are in ourselves, but the stronger we are in Him. The more I see of God, the less I become, the deeper is my confidence in Him. To become lowly, let God fill eye and heart. Where God is all, there is no time or place for man.

18. Stumblings

In many things we all stumble.'—Jas. 3:2

This word of God by James is the description of what man is, even the Christian, when he is not kept by grace. It serves to take away from us all hope in ourselves. (Rom. 7:14,23; Gal. 6:1) Now unto Him that is able to guard you from stumbling ... be glory, majesty, dominion, and power ... forevermore' (Jude 24,25). This word of God by Jude points to Him who can keep from falling, and stirs up the soul to ascribe to Him the honour and the power. It serves to confirm our hope in God. (2 Cor. 1:9; 1 Thess. 5:24; 2 Thess. 2:16,17; 3:3) Brethren, give the more diligence to make your calling and election sure: for if ye do these things, ye shall never stumble' (2 Pet. 1:10). This word of God by Peter teaches us the way in which we can become partakers of the keeping of the Almighty: the confirmation of our election by God in a godlike walk (see verses. 4,8,11). It serves to lead us into diligence and conscientious watchfulness. (Matt. 26:41; Luke 12:35; 1 Pet. 1:13; 5:8-10)

For the young Christian, it is often a difficult question what he ought to think of his stumblings. On this point, he ought especially to be on his guard against two errors. Some become dispirited when they stumble: they think that their surrender was not sincere, and lose their confidence towards God. (Heb. 3:6,14; 10:35) Others again take it too lightly. They think that it cannot be otherwise: they concern themselves little with stumblings, and continue to live in them. (Rom. 6:1; Gal. 2:18; 3:3) Let us take these words of God to teach us what we ought to think of our stumblings. There are three lessons.

Let no stumblings discourage you. You are called to perfectness: yet this comes not at once: time and patience are needful for it. Therefore James says: Let patience have its perfect work that ye may be perfect and entire. (Matt. 5:48; 2 Tim. 3:17; Heb. 13:20,21; Jas. 1:4; 1 Pet. 5:10) Think not that your surrender was not sincere; acknowledge only how weak you still are. Think not also that you must only continue stumbling: acknowledge only how strong your Saviour is.

Let stumbling rouse you to faith in the mighty keeper. It is because you have not relied on Him with a sufficient faith that you have stumbled. (Matt. 14:31; 17:20) Let stumbling drive you to Him. The first thing that you must do with a stumbling is: go with it to your Jesus. Tell it out to Him. (Ps. 38:18; 56:6; 1 John 1:9; 2:1) Confess it, and receive forgiveness. Confess it, and commit yourself with your weakness to Him, and reckon on Him to keep you. Sing continually the song: To Him that is mighty to keep you, be the glory.'

And then, let stumbling make you very prudent. (Prov. 28:14; Phil. 2:12; 1 Pet. 1:17,18) By faith you shall strive and overcome. In the power of your keeper and the joy and security of His help, you shall have courage to watch. The firmer you make your election, the stronger the certitude that He has chosen you, and will not let you go, the more conscientious shall you become, to live in all things only for Him, in Him, through Him. (2 Chron 20:15; Ps. 18:30,37; 44:5,9; John 5:4,5; Rom. 11:20; 2 Cor. 1:24; Phil. 2:13) Doing this, the word of God says, you shall never stumble.

Lord Jesus, a sinner who is ready to stumble every moment would givehonour to Thee, who art mighty to keep from stumbling: Thine is themight and the power: I take Thee as my keeper. I look to Thy lovewhich has chosen me, and wait for the fulfilment of Thy word: Yeshall never stumble.' Amen.

1. Let your thoughts about what the grace of God can do for you, be taken only from the word of God. Our natural expectations—that we must just always be stumbling—are wrong. They are strengthened by more than one thing. There is secret unwillingness to surrender everything. There is the example of so many sluggish Christians. There is the unbelief that cannot quite understand that God will really keep us. There is the experience of so many disappointments, when we have striven in our own power.

2. Let no stumbling be tolerated, for the reason that it is trifling.

19. Jesus The Keeper

The Lord is Thy keeper: ... The Lord shall keep thee from all evil; ... He shall keep thy soul.'—Ps. 121:4,7

I know Him whom I have believed, and I am persuaded that He is able to guard that which I have committed unto Him against that day.'—2 Tim. 1:12

For young disciples of Christ who are still weak, there is no lesson that is more necessary than this, that the Lord has not only received them, but that He will also keep them. (Gen. 28:15; Deut. 7:9; 32:10; Ps. 27:8; 89:33,34; Rom. 12:2,29) The lovely name, the Lord Thy keeper,' must for this end be carried in the heart, until the assurance of an Almighty keeping becomes as strong with us as it was with Paul, when he spake that glorious word: I know Him in whom I have believed, and I am persuaded that He is able to guard that which I have committed unto Him against that day.' Come and learn this lesson from him.

Learn from his to deposit your pledge with Jesus. Paul had surrendered himself, body and soul, to the Lord Jesus: that was His pledge which he had deposited with the Lord. You have also surrendered yourselves to the Lord, but perhaps not with the clear understanding that it is in order to be kept every day. Do this now daily. Deposit your soul with Jesus as a costly pledge that He will keep secure. Do this same thing with every part of your life. Is there something that you cannot rightly hold—your heart, because it is too worldly; (Ps. 31:6; Jer. 31:33) your tongue, because it is too idle; (Ps. 51:17; 141:3) your temper, because it is too passionate; (Ps. 119:165; Jer. 26:3,4; John 14:27; Phil. 4:6,7; 2 Thess. 3:16) your calling to confess the Lord, because you are too weak? (Isa. 50:7; Jer. 1:9; Matt. 10:19,20; Luke 26:15) Learn, then, to deposit it as a pledge for keeping with Jesus, in order that He may fulfil in you the promise of God about it. You often pray and strive too much in vain against a sin: it is because, although this is done with God's help, you would be the person who would overcome. No: entrust the matter wholly to Jesus: the battle is not yours, but God's. (Ex. 14:14; Deut. 3:22; 20:4 2 Chron. 20:15) Leave it in His hands: believe in Him to do it for you: This is the victory that hath overcome the world, even your faith.' (Matt. 9:23; 1 John 5:3,4) But you must first place it wholly out of your hands in His.

Learn from Paul to set your confidence only on the power of Jesus. I am persuaded that He is able to keep my pledge. You have an almighty Jesus to keep you. Faith keeps itself occupied only with His omnipotence. (Gen. 17:1; 18:14; Jer. 32:17,27; Matt. 8:27; 28:18; Luke 1:37,49; 18:27; Rom. 4:21; Heb. 11:18) Let your faith especially be strengthened in what God is able to do for you. (Rom. 4:21; 14:4; 2 Cor. 9:8; 2 Tim. 1:12) Expect with certainty from Him that He will do for you great and glorious things, entirely above your own strength. See in the Holy Scriptures how constantly the power of God was the ground of the trust of His people. Take these words and hide them in your heart. Let the power of Jesus fill your soul. Ask only: What is my Jesus able to do?' What you really trust Him with, He is able to keep. (John 13:1; 1 Cor. 1:8,9)

And learn also from Paul where he obtained the assurance that this power would keep his pledge: it was in his knowledge of Jesus. I know Him whom I have believed:' therefore I am assured. (John 10:14,28; Gal. 2:20; 2 Tim. 4:18; 1 John 2:13,14) You can trust the power of Jesus, if you know that He is yours, if you hold converse with Him as your friend. Then you can say: I know whom I have believed: I know that he holds my very dear: I know and am assured that He is able to keep my pledge.' So runs the way to the full assurance of faith: Deposit your pledge with Jesus; give yourselves wholly, give everything, into His hands; think much on His might, and reckon upon Him; and live with Him so that you may always know who He is in whom you have believed.

Young disciples of Christ, pray, receive this word: The Lord is thy keeper.' For every weakness, every temptation, learn to deposit your soul with Him as a pledge. You can reckon upon it, you can shout joyfully over it: The Lord shall keep you from all evil. (Josh. 1:9; Ps. 23:4; Rom. 8:35,39)

Holy Jesus, I take Thee as my keeper. Let Thy name, The Lord thykeeper,' sound as a song in my heart the whole day. Teach me inevery need to deposit my case as a pledge with Thee, and to beassured that Thou art able to keep it. Amen.

1. There was once a woman who for years long, and with much prayer, had striven against her temper, but could not obtain the victory. On a certain day she resolved not to come out of her room until by earnest prayer she had the power to overcome. She went out in the opinion that she should succeed. Scarcely had she been in the household, when something gave her offense and caused her to be angry. She was deeply ashamed, burst into tears, and hastened back to her room. A daughter, who understood the way of faith better than she, went to her and said, Mother, I have observed your conflict: may I tell you what I think the hindrance is?' Yes, my child,' Mother, you struggle against temper, and pray that the Lord may help you to overcome. This is wrong. The Lord must do it alone. You must give temper wholly into His hands: then He takes it wholly, and He keeps you.' The mother could not at first understand this, but later it was made plain to her. And she enjoyed the blessedness of the life in which Jesus keeps us, and we by faith have the victory. Do you understand this?

2. The Lord must help me to overcome sin:' the expression is altogether outside of the New Testament. The grace of God in the soul does not become a help to us. He will do everything: The Spirit has made me free from the law of sin.'

3. When you surrender anything to the Lord for keeping, take heed to two things: that you give it wholly into His hands; and that you have it there. Let Him have it wholly: He will carry out your case gloriously.

20. Power And Weakness

He hath said unto me, My power is made perfect in weakness. Therefore will I glory in my weaknesses, that the strength of Christ may rest upon me. Wherefore I take pleasure in weaknesses: for when I am weak, then am I strong.'—2 Cor. 12:9,10

There is almost no word that is so imperfectly understood in the Christian life as the word weakness. Sin and shortcoming, sluggishness and disobedience, are set to the account of our weakness. With this appeal to weakness, the true feeling of guilt and the sincere endeavour after progress are impossible. How, pray, can I be guilty, when I do not do what it is not in my power to do? The Father cannot demand of His child what He can certainly do independently. That, indeed, was done by the law under the Old Covenant; but that the Father, under the New Covenant, does not do. He requires of us nothing more than what He has prepared for us power to do in His Holy Spirit. The new life is a life in the power of Christ through the Spirit.

The error of this mode of thinking is that people estimate their weakness, not too highly, but too meanly. They would still do something by the exercise of all their powers, and with the help of God. They know not that they must be nothing before God. (Rom. 4:4,5; 11:6; 1 Cor. 1:27,28) You think that you have still a little strength, and that the Father must help you by adding something of His own power to your feeble energy. This thought is wrong. Your weakness appears in the fact that you can do nothing. It is better to speak of utter inability—that is what the Scriptures understand by the word weakness.' Apart from me ye can do nothing.' In us is no power.' (2 Chron. 16:9; 20:12; John 5:19; 15:5; 2 Cor. 1:9)

Whenever the young Christian acknowledges and assents to this his weakness, then he learns to understand the secret of the power of Jesus. He then sees that he is not to wait and pray to become stronger, to feel stronger. No: in his inability, he is to have the power of Jesus. By faith he is to receive it; he is to reckon that it is for him, and that Jesus Himself will work in and by him. (John 15:5; 1 Cor 1:24; 15:10; Eph. 1:18,19; Col. 1:11) It then becomes clear to him what the Lord means when He says, My power is made perfect in your weakness.' He knows to return the answer, When I am weak, then am I—yea, then am I—strong.' Yea, the weaker I am, the stronger I become. And he learns to sing with Paul, I shall glory in my weaknesses.' I take pleasure in weaknesses.' We rejoice when we are weak.' (2 Cor. 11:30; 12:9,11; 13:4,9)

It is wonderful how glorious that life of faith becomes for him who is content to have nothing, or feel nothing, in himself, and always to live on the power of his Lord. He learns to understand what a joyful thing it is to know God as his strength. The Lord is my strength and song.' (Ps. 89:18; 118:14; Jer. 12:2) He lives in what the Psalms so often express: I love Thee, O Lord, my strength;' I will sing of Thy strength: unto Thee, O my strength, will I sing praises.' (Ps. 18:2; 28:7,8; 31:5; 43:2; 46:2; 59:17,18; 62:8; 81:2) He understands what is meant when a psalm says, Give strength to the Lord: the Lord will give strength to His people;' and when another says, Give strength to God: the God of Israel, He giveth strength and power to His people.' (Ps. 29:1,11; 68:35,36) When we give or ascribe all the power to God, then He gives it to us again.

'I have written unto you, young men, because ye are strong, and the word of God abideth in you, and ye have overcome the Evil

One.' The Christian is strong in his Lord: (Ps. 71:16; 1 John 2:14) not sometimes strong and sometimes weak, but always weak, and therefore always strong. He has merely to know and use his strength trustfully. To be strong is a command, a behest that must be obeyed. On obedience there comes more strength. Be strong ... and He shall strengthen thine heart.' In faith the Christian must simply obey the command, Be strong in the Lord, and in the power of His might.' (Ps. 27:14; 31:25; Isa. 40:31; Eph. 6:10)

The God of the Lord Jesus, the Father of glory give unto us thespirit of wisdom and of revelation in the knowledge of Jesus, thatwe may know what is the exceeding greatness of His power to uswardwho believe. Amen.

1. So long as the Christian thinks of the service of God or of sanctification as something that is hard and difficult, he will make no progress in it. He must see that this very thing is for him impossible. Then he will cease still endeavouring to do something; he will surrender himself that Christ may work all in him. See these thoughts set forth in detail in Professor Hofmeyr's book, Out of Darkness into Light: a Course of Instruction on Conversion, the Surrender of Faith, and Sanctification [1] (J.H. Rose, Cape Town), chapter third and following of the third part.

2. The complaint about weakness is often nothing else than an apology for our idleness. There is power to be obtained in Christ for those who will take the pains to have it.

3. Be strong in the Lord and in the power of His might.' Mind that. I must abide in the Lord and in the power of His might, then I become strong. To have His power I must have Himself. The strength is His, and continues His; the weakness continues mine. He, the Strong, works in me, the weak; I, the weak, abide by faith in Him, the Strong; so that I, in the self-same moment, know myself to be weak and strong.

4. Strength is for work. He who would be strong simply to be pious, will not be so. He who in his weakness begins to work for

the Lord, shall become strong.

[1] Professor N.J. Hofmeyr is senior professor of the Theological College of the Dutch Reformed Church, Stellenbosch, Cape Colony. The volume referred to has been recently published in English under the title, The Blessed Life: How to Find and Live It (J. Nisbet & Co.), (vide P. 185). —Translator

21. The Life Of Feeling

We walk by faith, not by sight.'—2 Cor. 5:7

Blessed are they that have not seen, and yet have believed.'—John 20:29

Said I not unto thee, that, if thou believedst, thou shouldest see the glory of God?'—John 11:40

In connection with your conversion there was no greater hindrance in your way than feeling. You thought, perhaps for years, that you must experience something, must feel and perceive something in yourselves. It was to you as if it were too hazardous thus simply, and without some feeling, to believe in the word, and be sure that God had received you, and that your sins were forgiven. But at last you have had to acknowledge that the way of faith, without feeling, was the way of the word of God. And it has been to you the way of salvation. Through faith alone have you been saved, and your soul has found rest and peace. (John 3:36; Rom. 3;28; 4:5,16; 5:1)

In the further life of the Christian there is no temptation that is more persistent and more dangerous than this same feeling. The word feeling' we do not find in Scripture, but what we call feeling' the Scripture calls seeing'. And it tells us without easing that not seeing, but believing, that believing right in opposition to what we see, gives salvation. Abraham, not being weak in faith, considered not his own body'. * Faith adheres simply to what God says. The unbelief that would see shall not see; the faith that will not see, but has enough in God, shall see the glory of God. (2 Chron. 7:2; Ps. 2713; Isa. 7:9; Matt. 14:30,31; Luke 5:5) The man who seeks for feeling, and mourns about it, shall not find it; the man who cares not for it shall have it overflowing. Whosoever would save his life shall lose it, and whosoever shall lose his life for my sake shall find it.' Faith in the word becomes later on sealed with true feeling by the Holy Spirit. (John 12:25; Gal. 3:2,14; Eph. 1:13)

Child of God, learn to live by faith. Let it be fixed with you that faith is God's way to a blessed life. When there is no feeling of liveliness in prayer, when you feel cold and dull in the inner chamber, live by faith. Let your faith look upon Jesus as near, upon His power and faithfulness, and, though you have nothing to bring to Him, believe that He will give you all. Feeling always seeks something in itself; faith keeps itself occupied with what Jesus is. (Rom. 4:20,21; 2 Tim. 1:12; Heb. 9:5,6; Jas. 3:16; 6:16) When you read the word, and have no feeling of interest or blessing, read it yet again in faith. The word will work and bring blessing; the word worketh in those that believe.' When you feel no love, believe in the love of Jesus, and say in faith that He knows that you still love Him. When you have no feeling of gladness, believe in the inexpressible joy that there is in Jesus for you. Faith is blessedness, and will give joy to those who are not concerned about the self-sufficiency that springs from joy, but about the glorification of God that springs from faith. (Rom. 15:13; Gal. 2:20; 1 Pet. 1:5,7,8) Jesus will surely fulfil His word: Blessed are they that have not seen, and yet have believed.' Said I not unto thee, that, if thou believedst, thou shouldest see the glory of God?'

Betwixt the life of feeling and the life of faith the Christian has to choose every day. Happy is he who, once for all, has made the firm choice, and every morning renews the choice, not to seek or listen for feeling, but only to walk by faith, according to the will of God. The faith that keeps itself occupied with the word, with what

God has said, and, through the word, with God Himself and Jesus His Son, shall taste the blessedness of a life in God above. Feeling seeks and aims at itself; faith honours God, and shall be honoured by Him. Faith pleases God, and shall receive from Him the witness in the heart of the believer that he is acceptable to God.

Lord God, the one, the only, thing that Thou desirest of Thychildren is that they should trust Thee, and that they should alwayshold converse with Thee in that faith. Lord, let it be the onething in which I seek my happiness, to honour and to please Thee bya faith that firmly holds Thee, the Invisible, and trusts Thee inall things. Amen.

1. There is indeed something marvelous in the new life. It is difficult to make it clear to the young Christian. The Spirit of God teaches him to understand it after he perseveres in grace. Jesus has laid the foundation of that life in the first word of the Sermon on the Mount: Blessed are the poor in spirit, for theirs is the kingdom of heaven'; a feeling of deep poverty and of royal riches, of utter weakness and of kingly might, exist together in the soul. To have nothing in itself, to have all in Christ—that is the secret of faith. And the true secret of faith is to bring this into exercise, and, in hours of barrenness and emptiness, still to know that we have all in Christ.

2. Forget not that the faith, of which God's word speaks so much, stands not only in opposition to works, but also in opposition to feeling, and therefore that for a pure life of faith you must cease to seek your salvation, not only in works, but also in faith. Therefore let faith always speak against feeling. When feeling says, In myself, I am sinful; I am dark; I am weak; I am poor; I am sad;' let faith say. In Christ, I am holy; I am light; I am strong; I am rich; I am joyful.'

22. The Holy Ghost

And because ye are sons, God sent forth the Spirit of His Son into our hearts, crying, Abba, Father.'—Gal. 4:6

The great gift of the Father, through whom He obtained salvation and brought it near to us, is the Son. On the other hand, the great gift of the Son, whom He sends to us from the Father, to apply to us an inner and effectual salvation, is the Holy Spirit. (John 7:38; 14:16,26; Acts 1:4; 2:33; 1 Cor. 3:16) As the Son reveals and glorifies the Father, so the Spirit reveals and glorifies the Son. (John 15:26; 16:14,15; 1 Cor. 2:8,12; 12:3) The Spirit is in us to transfer to us the life and the salvation that are prepared in Jesus, and to make them wholly ours. (Job 14:17,21; Rom. 8:2; Eph. 3:17,19) Jesus who is in heaven is made present in us, dwells in us, by the Spirit. We have seen that in order to become partaker of Jesus there are always two things necessary: the knowledge of the sin that is in us, and of the redemption that is in Him. It is the Holy Spirit who continually promotes this double work in believers. He reproves and comforts, He convinces of sin and He glorifies Christ. (John 16:9,14)

The Spirit convinces of sin. He is the light and the fire of God, through whom sin is unveiled and consumed. He is the Spirit of judgment and of burning,' by whom God purifies His people. (Isa. 4:4; Zech. 12:10,11; Matt. 3:11,12) To the anxious soul who complains that he does not feel his sin deeply enough, we must often say that there is no limit as to how deep his repentance must be. He must come daily just as he is; the deepest conviction often times comes after conversion. To the young convert we have simply to say: let the Spirit who is in you convince you always of sin. Sin, which formerly you knew but by name, He will make you hate. Sin, which you had not seen in the hidden depths of your heart, He will make you know, and with shame confess. Sin, of which you fancied that it was not with you, and which you had judged severely in others, He will point out to you in yourself. (Ps. 139:7,23; Isa. 10:17; Matt. 7:5; Rom. 14:4; 1 Cor. 2:10; 14:24,25) And He will teach you with repentance and self-condemnation to cast yourself upon grace as entirely sinful, in order to be thereby redeemed and purified from it.

Beloved brother, the Holy Spirit is in you as the light and fire of God to unveil and to consume sin. The temple of God is holy, and this temple you are. Let the Holy Spirit in you have full mastery to point out and expel sin. (Ps. 19:13; 139:23; Mic. 3:8; 1 Cor. 3:17; 2 Cor. 3:17; 5:16) After He makes you know sin, He will at every turn make you know Jesus as your life and your sanctification.

And then shall the Spirit who rebukes also comfort. He will glorify Jesus in you, will take what is in Jesus and make it known to you. He will give you knowledge concerning the power of Jesus' blood to cleanse, (1 John 1:7; 5:6) and the power of Jesus' indwelling to keep. (John 14:21,23; Eph. 3:17; 1 John 3:24; 4:13) He will make you see how literally, how completely, how certainly Jesus is with you every moment, to do Himself all his own Jesus-work in you. Yea, in the Holy Spirit, the living, almighty, and ever-present Jesus shall be your portion; you shall also know this, and have the full enjoyment of it. The Holy Spirit will teach you to bring all your sin and sinfulness to Jesus, and to know Jesus with His complete redemption from sin as your own. As the Spirit of sanctification, He will drive out sin in order that He may cause Jesus to dwell in you. (Rom. 1:4; 5:5; 8:2,13; 1 Pet. 1:2)

Beloved young Christian, take time to understand and to become filled with the truth: the Holy Spirit is in you. Review all the assurances of God's word that this is so. (Rom. 8:14,16; 1 Cor. 6:19; 2 Cor. 1:22; 6:16; Eph. 1:13) Pray, think not for a moment of living as a Christian without the indwelling of the Spirit. Take pains to have your heart filled with the faith that the Spirit dwells in you, and will do His mighty work, for through faith the Spirit comes and works (Gal. 3:2,5,15; 5:5) Have a great reverence for the work of the Spirit in you. Seek Him every day to believe, to obey, to trust, and He will take and make known to you all that there is in Jesus. He will make Jesus very glorious to you and in you.

O my Father, I thank Thee for this gift which Jesus sent me fromThee, the Father. I thank Thee that I am now the temple of ThySpirit, and that He dwells in me. Lord, teach me to believe thiswith the whole heart, and to live in the world as one who knows thatthe Spirit of God is in him to lead him. Teach me to think withdeep reverence and filial awe on this, that God is in me. Lord, inthat faith I have the power to be holy. Holy Spirit, reveal to meall that sin is in me. Holy Spirit, reveal to me all that Jesus isin me. Amen.

1. The knowledge of the person and the work of the Holy Spirit is for us of just as much importance as the knowledge of the person and the work of Christ.

2. Concerning the Holy Spirit, we must endeavour especially to hold fast the truth that He is given as the fruit of the work of Jesus for us, that He is the power of the life of Jesus in us, and that through Him, Jesus Himself, with His full salvation, dwells in us.

3. In order to enjoy all this, we must be filled with the Spirit. This simply means, emptied of all else and full of Jesus. To deny ourselves, to take up the cross, to follow Jesus. Or rather, this is the way in which the Spirit leads us to His fulness. No one has the power to enter fully into the death of Jesus but he who is led by the Spirit. But He takes him that desires this by the hand and brings

him.

4. As the whole of salvation, the whole of the new life is by faith, so is this also true of the gift and the working of the Holy Spirit. By faith, not by works—not in feeling, do I receive Him, am I led by Him, am I filled with Him.

5. As clear and definite as my faith is in the work that Jesus only and alone finished for me, so clear and definite must faith be in the work that the Holy Spirit accomplishes in me, to work in me the willing and the performing of all that is necessary for my salvation.

23. The Leading Of The Spirit

As many as are led by the Spirit of God, these are sons of God. The Spirit Himself beareth witness with our spirit, that we are children of God.'—Rom. 8:14,16

It is the very same Spirit that leads us as children who also assures us that we are children. Without His leading there can be no assurance of our filiation. True full assurance of faith is enjoyed by him who surrenders himself entirely to the leading of the Spirit.

In what does this leading consist? Chiefly in this, that our whole hidden inner life is guided by Him to what it ought to be. This we must firmly believe. Our growth and increase, our development and progress, is not our work but His: we are to trust Him for this. As a tree or animal grows and becomes large by the spirit of life which God has given to it, so also does the Christian by the Spirit of life in Christ Jesus. (Hos. 14:6,7; Matt. 6:28; Mark 4:26,28; Luke 2:40; Rom. 8:2) We have to cherish the joyful assurance that the Spirit whom the Father gives to us does with divine wisdom and power guide our hidden life, and bring it where God will have it.

Then there are also special directions of this leading. He will lead you into all the truth,' When we read the word of God, we are to wait upon Him, to make us experience the truth, the essential power of what God says. He makes the word living and powerful. He leads us into a life corresponding to the word. (John 6:63,

14:26; 16:13; 1 Cor. 2:10,114; 1 Thess. 2:13)

When you pray, you can reckon upon His leading: The Spirit helpeth our infirmities.' He leads us to what we must desire. He leads us into the way in which we are to pray, trustfully, persistently, mightily. (Zech 12:10; Rom. 8:26,27; Jude 12,20)

In the way of sanctification it is He that will lead: He leads us in the path of righteousness. He leads us into all the will of God. (1 Cor. 6:19,20; 1 Pet 1:2,15)

In our speaking and working for the Lord, He will lead. Every child has the Spirit: every child has need of Him to know and to do the work of the Father. Without Him no child can please or serve the Father. The leading of the Spirit is the blessed privilege, the sure token, the only power of a child of God. (Matt. 10:20; Acts 1:8; Rom 8:9,13; Gal. 4:6; Eph. 1:13)

And how then can you fully enjoy this leading? The first thing that is necessary for this is faith. You must take time, young Christian, to have your heart filled with the deep and living consciousness that the Spirit is in you. Read all the glorious declarations of your Father in His word concerning what the Spirit is in you and for you, until the conviction wholly fills you that you are really a temple of the Spirit. Ignorance or unbelief on this point makes it impossible for the Spirit to speak in you and to lead you. Cherish an ever-abiding assurance that the Spirit of God dwells in you. (Acts. 19:2; Rom. 5:5; 1 Cor. 3:16; 2 Cor. 5:5 Gal. 3:5,14)

Then the second thing that is necessary is this: you are to hold yourself still, to attend to the voice of the Spirit. As the Lord Jesus acts, so does the Spirit. As the Lord Jesus acts, so does also the Spirit: He shall not cry nor lift up His voice.' He whispers gently and quietly: only the soul that sets itself very silently towards God can perceive His voice and guidance. When we become to a needless extent engrossed with the world, with its business, its cares, its enjoyments, its literature, its politics, the Spirit cannot lead us. When our service of God is a bustling and working in our own wisdom and strength, the Spirit cannot be heard in us. It is the weak, the simple, who are willing to have themselves taught in humility, that receive the leading of the Spirit. Sit down every morning, sit down often in the day, to say: Lord Jesus, I know nothing, I will be silent: let the Spirit lead me. (1 Chron. 19:12; Ps. 62; 2,6; 131:2; Isa. 43:2; Hab. 2:20; Zech. 4:6 Acts 1:4)

And then: be obedient. Listen to the inner voice, and do what it says to you. Fill your heart every day with the word, and when the Spirit puts you in mind of what the word says, betake yourself to the doing of it. So you become capable of further teaching: it is to the obedient that the full blessing of the Spirit is promised. (John 14:15,16; Acts 5:32

Young Christian, know that you are a temple of the Spirit, and that it is only through the daily leading of the Spirit that you can walk as a child of God, with the witness that you are pleasing the Father.

Precious Saviour, imprint this lesson deeply on my mind. The HolySpirit is in me. His leading is every day and everywhereindispensable for me. I cannot hear His voice in the word when I donot wait silently upon Him. Lord, let a holy circumspectness keepwatch over me, that I may always walk as a pupil of the Spirit.Amen.

1. It is often asked: How do I know that I shall continue standing, that I shall be kept, that I shall increase? The question dishonours the Holy Spirit—is the token that you do not know Him or do not trust Him. The question indicates that you are seeking the secret of strength for perseverance in yourself, and not in the Holy Spirit, your heavenly Guide.

2. As God sees to it, that every moment there is air for me to breathe, so shall the Holy Spirit unceasingly maintain life in the hidden depths of my soul. He will not break off his own work.

3. From the time that we receive the Holy Spirit, we have nothing to do but to honour his work: to keep our hands off from

it, and to trust Him, and to let Him work.

4. The beginning and the end of the work of the Spirit is to reveal Jesus to me, and to cause me to abide in Him. As soon as I would fain look after the work of the Spirit in me, I hinder Him: He cannot work when I am not willing to look upon Jesus.

5. The voice of the Father, the voice of the good Shepherd, the voice of the Holy Spirit is very gentle. We must learn to become deaf to other voices, to the world and its news of friends and their thoughts, to our own Ego and its desires: then shall we distinguish the voice of the Spirit. Let us often set ourselves silent in prayer, entirely silent, to offer up our will and our thoughts, and, with our eye upon Jesus, to keep ear and heart open for the voice of the Spirit.

24. Grieving The Spirit

Grieve not the Holy Spirit of God, in whom you were sealed unto the day of redemption.'—Eph. 4:30

It is by the Holy Spirit that the child of God is sealed: separated and stamped and marked as the possession of God. This sealing is not a dead or external action that is finished once for all. It is a living process, which has power in the soul, and gives firm assurance of faith, only when it is experienced through the life of the Spirit in us. On this account we are to take great care not to grieve the Spirit: in Him alone can you have every day the joyful certitude and the full blessing of your childship. [2] It is the very same Spirit that leads us who witnesses with our spirit that we are children of God. And how can any one grieve the Spirit? Above all by yielding to sin. He is the Holy Spirit, given to sanctify us, and, for every sin from which the blood cleanses us, to fill us with the holy life of God, with God. Sin grieves Him. (Isa. 53:10; Acts. 7:51; Heb. 10:29) For this reason the word of God presently states by name the sins against which above all we are to be on our guard. Mark only the four great sins that Paul mentions in connection with our text.

There is first lying. There is no single sin that in the Bible is so brought into connection with the devil as lying. Lying is from hell, and it goes on to hell. God is the God of truth. And the Holy Spirit cannot possibly carry forward His blessed working in a man or woman that lies, that is insincere, that does injury to the truth. Young Christian, review with care what the word of God says about lying and liars, and pray God that you may never speak anything but the literal truth. Grieve not the Holy Spirit of God. (Ps. 5:7; Prov. 12:22; 21:28; John 8:44; Rev. 21:8,27; 22:15)

Then there is anger. Let all bitterness, and wrath, and anger, and clamour, and evil-speaking, be put away from you.' Hastiness, proneness to anger, sin of temper is, along with lying, the most common sin by which the Christian is kept back from increase in grace. (Matt. 5:22,26,27; 1 Cor. 1:10,11; 3:3; 13:1,3; Gal. 5:5; 15:21,26; Col. 3:8,12; 1 Thess. 5:15; Jas. 3:14) Christian, let all passionateness by put away from you: this follows on the command not to grieve the Spirit. Believe that the Holy Spirit, the great power of God, is in you. Surrender yourself every day to His indwelling, in faith that Jesus can keep you by Him: He will make and keep you gentle. Yea, believe, I pray you, in the power of God, and of Jesus and of the Holy Spirit to overcome temper. (Matt. 11:29; 1 Cor. 6:19,20; Gal. 6:1; Eph. 2:16,17; Col. 1:8; 2 Tim. 1:12) Confess the sin: God shall cleanse you from it. Grieve not the Holy Spirit of God.

Then there is stealing: all sin against the property or possession of my neighbour: all deception and dishonesty in trade, whereby I do wrong to my neighbour, and seek my own advantage at his cost. The law of Christ is love whereby I seek the advantage of my neighbour as well as my own. O the love of money and property, which is inseparable from self-seeking—it is incompatible with the leading of the Holy Spirit. The Christian must be a man who is known as honest to the back-bone, righteous, and loving his neighbour as himself. (Luke 6:31; Rom. 13:10; 1 Thess. 4:6)

Then says the apostle: no corrupt speech—but such as is good for edifying as the case may be.' Even the tongue of God's child belongs to his Lord. He must be known by his mode of speech. By his speaking, he can grieve or please the Spirit. The sanctified tongue is a blessing not only to his neighbours but to the speaker himself. Foul talk, idle words, foolish jests—they grieve the Holy Spirit. They make it impossible for the Spirit to sanctify and to comfort and to fill the heart with the love of God. (Prov. 10:19, 20,21,31; 18:20; Eccles. 5:1,2; Matt. 12:36; Eph. 5:4; Jas. 3:9,10)

Young Christian, I pray you, grieve not the Holy Spirit of God by these or other sins. If you have committed such sins, confess them, and God will cleanse you from them. By the Holy Spirit you are sealed if you would walk in the stability and joy of faith, listen to the word: Grieve not the Holy Sprit of God.'

Lord God, my Father in heaven, do, I pray thee, cause me tounderstand what marvelous grace Thou art manifesting to me, in thatThou hast given to me Thy Holy Spirit in my heart. Lord, let thisfaith by the argument and the power for cleansing me from everysin. Holy Jesus, sanctify me, that in my thinking, speaking, acting—in all things, Thine image may appear. Amen.

1. The thought of the Christian about this word, Grieve not the Holy Spirit' is a touchstone as to whether he understands the life of faith.

For some it is a word of terror and fear. A father once brought a child to the train to go on a journey with the new governess, with whom she was to remain. Before her departure he said: I hear that she is very sensitive and takes things much amiss: take care that you do nothing to grieve her.' The poor child had no pleasant journey: it appeared to her very grievous to be in anxious fear of one who was so prone to take anything wrong amiss.

This is the view of the Holy Spirit which many have: a Being whom it is difficult to satisfy, who thinks little of our weakness, and who, even though we take pains, is discontented when our work is not perfect.

2. Another father also brought his daughter to the train to go on a journey, and to be a time from home: but in company with her mother, whom she loved very dearly. You are to be a good child,'

said the father, and do everything to please your mamma; otherwise you shall grieve her and me.' Oh, certainly, papa!' was the joyful answer of the child. For she felt so happy to be with her mother, and was willing to do her utmost to be agreeable to her.

There are children of God to whom the Holy Spirit is so well known in His tender, helpful love, and the Comforter and the Good Spirit, that the word, Grieve not the spirit of God' has for them a gentle, encouraging power. May our fear to grieve Him always be the tender childlike fear of trustful love.

[2] Kindschap—a word coined by the writer to express the relation of a child. Our childhood expresses rather the state or stage of child-life.—Translator

25. Flesh And Spirit

And I, brethren, could not speak unto you as unto spiritual, but as unto carnal, as unto babes in Christ.'—1 Cor. 3:1

I am carnal, sold under sin: to will is present with me, but to do that which is good is not. The law of the Spirit of life in Christ Jesus made me free from the law of sin and of death. Ye are not in the flesh, but in the Spirit, if so be that the Spirit of God dwelleth in you.'—Rom. 7:14,18; 8:2,9

Having begun in the Spirit, are ye now perfected in the flesh? If ye are led by the Spirit, ye are not under the law. If we live by the Spirit, by the Spirit let us also walk.'—Gal. 3:3; 5:18,25

It is of great importance for the young Christian to understand that there are in him two natures, which strive against one another. (Gal. 5:17,24,25; 6:8; Eph. 4:22,24; Col. 3:9,10; 1 Pet. 4:2) If we weigh the texts noted above, we shall see that the word of God teaches us the following truths on this point.

Sin comes from the flesh: the reason why the Christian still does sin is that he yields to the flesh and does not walk by the Spirit. Every Christian has the Spirit and lives by the Spirit, but every Christian does not walk by the Spirit. If he walks by the Spirit, he will not fulfil the desires of the flesh. (Rom. 8:7; 1 Cor. 3:1,3; Gal. 5:16,25)

So long as there are still in the Christian strife and envy, the word of God calls him carnal. He would indeed do good, but he cannot: he does what he would not, because he still strives in his own strength and not in the power of the Spirit. (Rom. 7:18; 1 Cor. 3:3; Gal. 5:15,26)

The flesh remains under the law, and seeks to obey the law. But through the flesh the law is powerless, and the endeavour to do good is vain. Its language is: I am carnal, sold under sin: to will is present with me, but to do that which is good is not.' (Rom. 6:14;15; 7:4,6; 8:3,8; Gal. 5:18; 6:12,13; Heb. 7:18; 8:9,13)

This is not the condition in which God would have his child remain. The word says: It is God that worketh in you, both to will and to work.' [3] The Christian must not only live by the Spirit, but also walk by the Spirit. He must be a spiritual man, and abide entirely under the leading of the Spirit. (Rom. 8:14; 1 Cor. 2:15; 3:1; Gal. 6:1) If he thus walks, he will no longer do what he would not. He will no longer remain in the condition of Romans 7, as a new-born babe, still seeking to fulfil the law, but in Romans 8, a one who through the Spirit is made free from the law with its commandment, do this,' which gives no power, but brings death, and who walks, not in the oldness of the letter, but in the newness of the Spirit. (Rom. 7:6; 8:2,13)

There are Christians that begin with the Spirit, but end with the flesh. They are converted, born again through the Spirit, but fall unconsciously into a life in which they endeavour to overcome sin and be holy through their own exertion, through doing their best. They ask God to help them in these their endeavours, and think that this is faith. They do not understand what it is to say: In me, that is, in my flesh, dwelleth no good thing,' and that therefore they are to cease from their own endeavours, in order to do God's will, wholly and only through the Spirit. (Rom. 7:18; Gal. 3:3; 4:9; 5:4,7)

Child of God, pray, learn what it is to say of yourself, just as you are, even after the new birth: I am carnal, sold under sin.' Endeavour no longer to be doing your best, and to be praying to

God, and to be trusting Him to help you. No: learn to say: The law of the Spirit of life in Christ Jesus made me free from the law of sin and of death.' Let your work every day be to have the Spirit work in you, to walk by the Spirit, and you shall be redeemed from the life of complaining, the good that I would I do not,' into a life of faith, in which it is God that worketh in you both to will and to do.

Lord God, teach me to acknowledge with all my heart that in me, thatis, in my flesh, dwelleth nothing good. Teach me also to cease fromevery thought, as if I could with my own endeavours serve or pleaseThee. Teach me to understand that the Spirit is the Comforter, whofrees me from all anxiety and fear about my own powerlessness, inorder that He may work the strength of Christ in me. Amen.

1. In order to understand the conflict betwixt flesh and Spirit, we must especially seek to have a clear insight into the connection between Rom. 7 and 8. In Rom. 7:6 Paul had spoken of the twofold way of serving God, the one in the oldness of the letter, the other in the newness of the Spirit. In Rom. 7:14.16 he describes the first, in Rom. 8:1-16 the second. This appears clearly when we observe that in ch. 7 he mentions the Spirit but once, the law more than twenty times; in Rom. 8:1-16, the Spirit sixteen times. In Rom. 7 we see the regenerate soul, just as he is in himself with his new nature, desirous, but powerless, to fulfil the law, mourning as one who is captive under the law of sin.' In Rom. 8 we hear him say, the law of the Spirit of life in Christ made me free from the law of sin.' Rom. 7 describes the ever-abiding condition of the Christian, contemplated as renewed, but not experiencing by faith the power of the Holy Spirit: Rom. 8 his life in the freedom which the Spirit of God really gives from the power of sin.

2. It is of very great importance to understand that the conflict between grace and works, between faith and one's own power, between the Holy Spirit and confidence in ourselves and the flesh, always continues to go on, not only in connection with conversion

and the reception of the righteousness of God, but even further, into a walk in this righteousness. On this account the Christian has to watch very carefully against the deep inclination of his heart still to work in his own behalf, when he sees in himself anything wrong or when he would follow after holiness, instead of always and only trusting in Jesus Christ, and so serving God in the Spirit.

3. In order to make clear the opposition between the two methods of serving God, let me adduce consecutively in their entirety the passages in which they are expressed with special distinctness. Compare them with care. Pray God for the Spirit in order to make you understand them. Take deeply to heart the lesson as to how you are to serve God well, and how not.

The circumcision of the heart, in the Spirit, not in the letter. (Rom. 2:29)

To him that worketh not but believeth, his faith is reckoned for righteousness. (Rom. 4:5)

Ye are not under the law but under grace. (Rom. 6:14)

We have been discharged from the law, so that we serve in newness of the Spirit and not in the oldness of the letter. (Rom. 7:6)

We know that the law is spiritual, but I am carnal, sold under sin. (Rom. 7:14)

The ordinance of the law is fulfilled in us, who walk not after the flesh but after the Spirit. (Rom. 8:4)

Ye received not the Spirit of bondage again to fear, but ye received the Spirit of adoption. (Rom. 8:15)

The righteousness which is of the law is: The man that doeth these things shall live by them? But the righteousness which is of faith saith thus, Say not in thine heart, Who shall ascend? Who shall descend? But what saith it? The word is nigh thee, in thy mouth and in thy heart. (Rom. 5:5-8)

If it is by grace, it is no more of works. (Rom. 11:6)

I could not speak unto you as unto spiritual, but as unto carnal, as unto babes in Christ. (1 Cor. 3:7)

I live; and yet no longer I, but Christ liveth in me. (Gal. 2:20)

The righteous shall live by faith; yet the law is not of faith: but the man that doeth these things shall live by them. (Gal. 3:11,12)

If the inheritance is of the law, it is no more of promise. (Gal. 3:19)

So that thou art no longer a bondservant, but a son. (Gal. 4:7)

Wherefore, brethren, we are not children of a handmaid, but of the free-woman. (Gal. 4:31)

Walk by the Spirit and ye shall not fulfil the lust of the flesh. (Gal. 5:16)

If ye are led by the Spirit, ye are not under the law. (Gal. 5:18)

Who worship by the Spirit of God and glory in Christ Jesus, and have no confidence in the flesh. (Phil. 3:3)

Another priest, who hath been made not after the law of a carnal commandment, but after the power of an endless life. (Heb. 8:16)

4. Beloved Christian, you have received the Holy Spirit from the Lord Jesus to reveal Him and His life in you, and to mortify the working of the body of sin. Pray much to be filled with the Spirit. Live in the joyful faith that the Spirit is in you, as your Comforter and Teacher, and that through Him all will come right. Learn by heart this text, and let it live in your heart and on your lips: We are the circumcision, who worship by the Spirit of God and glory in Christ Jesus, and have no confidence in the flesh.'

[3] The Dutch version has—'and to accomplish.'—Translator

26. The Life Of Faith

The righteous shall live by his faith.'—Hab. 2:4

We have been discharged from the law, so that we serve in newness of the Spirit, and not in the oldness of the letter.'—Rom. 7:6

I live; and yet no longer I, but Christ liveth in me: and that life which I now live in the flesh I live in faith, the faith which is in the Son of God, who loved me, and gave Himself up for me.'—Gal. 2:20

The word from Habakkuk is thrice quoted in the New Testament as the Divine representation of salvation in Christ by faith alone. (Rom. 1:17; Gal. 3:11; Heb. 10:38) But that word is oftentimes very imperfectly understood, as if it ran: Man shall on his conversion be justified by faith. The word includes this, but signifies much more. It says that the righteous shall live by faith: the whole life of the righteous, from moment to moment, shall be by faith. (Rom. 5:17,21; 6:11; 8:2; Gal. 2:20; 1 John 5:11,12)

We all know how sharp is the opposition which God in His word presents betwixt the grace that comes by faith and the law that works—demands. This is generally admitted with reference to justification. But that distinction holds just as much of the whole life of sanctification. The righteous shall live by faith alone, that is, shall have power to live according to the will of God. As at his conversion he found it necessary to understand that there was nothing good in him, and that he must receive grace as one that was powerless and godless, so must he as a believer just as clearly understand that in him there is nothing good, and that he must receive his power for good every moment from above. (Rom. 7:18; 8:2,13; Heb. 11:38) And his work must therefore be every morning and every hour to look up and believe and receive his power from above, out of his Lord in heaven. I am not to do what I can, and hope in the Lord to supply strength. No: as one who has been dead, who is literally able for nothing in himself, and whose life is in his Lord above, I am to reckon by faith on Him who will work in me mightily (Rom. 4:17; 2 Cor. 1:9; Col. 1:20; 2:3)

Happy the Christian who understands that his greatest danger every day is again to fall under the law, and to be fain to serve God in the flesh with his own strength. Happy when he discerns that he is not under the law which just demands and yet is powerless through the flesh, but is under grace where we have simply to receive what has been given. Happy when he fully appropriates for himself the promise of the Spirit who transfers all that is in Christ to him. Yea, happy when he understands what it is to live by faith, and to serve, not in the oldness of the letter, but in the newness of the Spirit. (Rom. 7:4,6; 12:5,6; Gal. 5:18; Phil. 3:3)

Let us make our own the words of Paul: they present to us the true life of faith: I have been crucified with Christ; yet I live.' My flesh, not only my sin, but my flesh, all that is of myself, my own living and willing my own power and working, have I given up to death. I Live no longer—of myself, I cannot. I will not live, or do anything. (John 15:4,5; 1 Cor. 15:10; 2 Cor. 12:10) Christ lives in me: He Himself, by His Spirit, is my power, and teaches and strengthens me to live as I ought to do. And that life which I now live in the flesh, I live by faith in Him: my great work is to reckon upon Him to work in Him, as well the willing as the accomplishment.

Young Christian, let this life of faith be your faith.

O my Lord Jesus, Thou art my life: yea, my life. Thou livest in me,and art willing to take my whole life at Thine own charges. And mywhole life may daily be a joyful trust and experience that Thou artworking all in me. Precious Lord, to that life of faith will Isurrender myself. Yea, to Thee I surrender myself, to teach me andto reveal Thyself fully in me. Amen.

1. Do you discern the error of the expression—if the Lord helps me—the Lord must help me? In natural things we speak thus, for we have a certain measure of power, and the Lord will increase it. But the New Testament never uses the expression help' of the grace of God in the soul. We have absolutely no power—God is not to help us, because we are weak: no, He is to give His life and His power in us as entirely impotent. He that discerns this aright will learn to live by faith alone.

2. Without faith it is impossible to please God'; All that is not of faith is sin.' Such works of the Spirit of God teach us how really every deed and disposition of our life is to be full of faith.

3. Hence our first work every day is anew to exercise faith in Jesus as our life; to believe that He dwells in us, and will do all for us and in us. This faith must be the mood of our soul the whole day. This faith cannot be maintained except in the fellowship and nearness of Jesus Himself.

4. This faith has its power in the mutual surrender of Jesus and the believer to each other. Jesus first gives Himself wholly for us. The believer gives himself wholly in order to be taken into possession and guided by Jesus. Then the soul cannot even doubt if He will do all for it.

27. The Might Of Satan

Simon, Simon, behold, Satan asked to have you, that he might sift you as wheat: but I made supplication for thee, that thy faith fail not.'—Luke 22:31,32

There is nothing that makes an enemy so dangerous as the fact that he remains hidden or forgotten. Of the three great enemies of the Christian, the world, the flesh, and the devil, the last is the most dangerous, not only because it is he that, strictly speaking, lends to the others what power they have, but also because he is not seen, and, therefore, little known or feared. The devil has the power of darkness: he darkens the eyes, so that men do not know him. He surrounds himself with darkness, so that he is not observed. Yea, he has even the power to appear as an angel of light. (Matt. 4:6; 2 Cor. 4:4; 11:14) It is by the faith that recognizes things unseen that the Christian is to endeavour to know Satan, even as the Scripture has revealed him.

When the Lord Jesus was living upon earth, His great work was to overcome Satan. When at His baptism He was filled with the Spirit, this fulness of the Spirit brought him into contact with Satan as head of the world of evil spirits, to combat him and to overcome him. (Matt. 4:1,10) After that time the eyes of the Lord were always open to the power and working of Satan. In all sin and misery He saw the revelation of the mighty kingdom of the very same superior, the evil one. Not only in the demoniacs, but also in the sick, He saw the enemy of God and man. (Matt. 12:28; Mark 4:15; Luke 13:16; Acts. 10:38) In the advice of Peter to avoid the cross, and in his denial of his Lord, where we should think of the revelation of the natural character of Peter, Jesus saw the work of Satan. (Matt. 26:23; Luke 22:31,32) In His own suffering, where we rather speak of the sin of man and the permission of God, Jesus perceives the power of darkness. His whole work in living and in dying was to destroy the works of Satan, as He shall also at His second coming utterly bruise Satan himself. (Luke 10:18; 22:3,53; John 12:31; 14:30; 16:11; Rom. 16:20; Col. 2:15; 2 Thess. 2:8,9; 1 John 3:8)

His word to Peter, compared with the personal experience of the Lord, gives us a fearful insight into the work of the enemy. Satan hath eagerly desired you,' says Jesus. As a roaring lion, he walketh about, seeking whom he may devour,' says Peter himself later on. (1 Cor. 7:5; 2 Cor. 2:10; 1 Pet. 5:8) He has no unlimited power, but he is always eager to make use of every weak or unguarded moment. That he might sift you as wheat:' what a picture! This world, yea, even the Church of Christ, is the threshing-floor of Satan. The corn belongs to God; the chaff is his own. He sifts and sifts continually, and all that falls through with the chaff he endeavours to take for himself. And many a Christian is there who does fall through in a terrible fashion, and who, were it not for the intercession of his Lord, would perish for ever. (1 Cor. 5:5; 1 Tim. 1:20)

Satan has more than one sieve. The first is generally wordly-mindedness—the love of the world. Many a one is pious in his time of poverty, but when he becomes rich, he again eagerly strives to win the world. Or in the time of conversion and awakening he appears very zealous, but through the care of the world he is led astray. (Matt. 4:9; 8:22; 1 Tim. 6:9,10; 2 Tim. 4:10)

A second sieve is self-love and self-seeking. Whenever any one does not give himself undividedly to serve his Lord and his neighbour, and to love his neighbour in the Lord, it soon appears that the principal token of a disciple is lacking in him. It will be manifest that many a one, with a fair profession of being devoted to the service of God, fails utterly on this point, and must be reckoned with the chaff. Lovelessness is the sure token of the power of Satan. (John 8:44; 1 John 3:10,15; 4:20)

Yet another sieve, a very dangerous one, is self-confidence. Under the name of following the Spirit, one may listen to the thoughts of his own heart. He is zealous for the Lord, but with a carnal zeal, in which the gentleness of the Lamb of God is not seen. Without being observed, the movements of the flesh mingle with the workings of the Spirit, and while he boasts that he is overcoming Satan, he is being secretly ensnared by him. (Gal. 3:3; 5:13)

O it is a serious life here upon the earth, where God gives permission for Satan to set his threshing floor even in the Church. Happy are they who with deep humility, with fear and trembling, distrust themselves. Our only security is in the intercession and guidance of Him who overcame Satan. (Eph. 6:10,12,16) Far be from us the idea that we know all the depths of Satan, and are a match for all his cunning stratagems. It is in the region of the spirit, in the invisible, that he works and has power, as well as in the visible. Let us fear lest, while we have known and overcome him in the visible, he should prevail over us in the spiritual. May our only security be the conviction of our frailty and weakness, our confidence in Him who certainly keeps the lowly in heart.

Lord Jesus, open our eyes to know our enemy and his wiles. Cause us to see him and his realm, that we may dread all that is of him. And open our eyes to see how Thou hast overcome him, and how in Thee we are invincible. O teach us what it is to be in Thee, to mortify all that is of the mere Ego and the will of the flesh, and to be strongin weakness and lowliness. And teach us to bring into prayer theconflict of faith against every stronghold of Satan, because we knowthat Thou wilt bruise him under our feet. Amen.

1. What comfort does the knowledge of the existence of Satan give us? We know then that sin is derived from a foreign power which has thrust itself into our nature, and does not naturally belong to us. We know besides that he has been entirely vanquished by the Lord Jesus, and thus has no power over us so long as we abide trustfully in Christ.

2. The whole of this world, with all that is in it, is under the domination of Satan: therefore there is nothing, even what appears good and fair, that may not be dangerous for us. In all things, even in what is lawful and right, we must be led and sanctified by the Spirit, if we would continue liberated from the power of Satan.

3. Satan is an evil spirit: only by the good Spirit, the Spirit of God, can we offer resistance to him. He works in the invisible: in order to combat him, we have, by prayer, to enter into the invisible. He is a mighty prince: only in the name of One who is mightier and in fellowship with Him can we overcome.

4. What a glorious work is labour for souls, for the lost, for drunkards, for heathen; a conflict to rescue them from the might of Satan. (Acts. 26:18)

5. In the Revelation the victory over Satan is ascribed to the blood of the Lamb. (Rev. 12:11) Christians have also testified that there is no power in temptation, because Satan readily retreats when one appeals to the blood, by which one knows that sin has been entirely expiated, and we are thus also wholly freed from his power.

28. The Conflict Of The Christian

Strive to enter in by the narrow door.'—Luke 13:24

Fight the good fight of the faith.'—1 Tim. 6:12

I have fought the good fight, I have finished the course, I have kept the faith.'—2 Tim. 4:7

These texts speak of a twofold conflict. The first is addressed to the unconverted: Strive to enter in by the narrow door.' Entrance by a door is the work of a moment: the sinner is not to strive to enter during his whole lifetime: he is to strive and do it immediately. He is not to suffer anything to hold him back; he must enter in. (Gen. 19:22; John 10:9; 2 Cor. 6:2; Heb. 4:6,7)

Then comes the second, the life-long conflict: by the narrow door I come upon the new way. On the new way there are still always enemies. Of this life-long conflict Paul says: I have fought the good fight, I have finished the course, I have kept the faith.' With respect to the continuous conflict, he gives the charge: Fight the good fight of faith.'

There is much misunderstanding about this twofold conflict. Many strive all their life against the Lord and His summons, and, because they are not at rest, but feel an inner conflict, they think that this is the conflict of a Christian. Assuredly not: this is the struggle against God of one who is not willing to abandon everything and surrender himself to the Lord. (Acts 5:39; 1 Cor. 10:22) This is not the conflict that the Lord would have. What He says is that the conflict is concerned with entering in: but not a conflict for long years. No: He desires that you should break through the enemies that would hold you back, and immediately enter in.

Then follows the second conflict, which endures for life. Paul twice calls this the fight of faith. The chief characteristic of it is faith. He who understands well that the principal element in the battle is to believe, and acts accordingly, does certainly carry off the palm: just as in another passage Paul says to the Christian combatant: Withal taking up the shield of faith, wherewith ye shall be able to quench all the fiery darts of the evil one.' (Eph. 6:16; 1 John 3:4,5)

And what then does it mean, this fight of faith'? That, while I strive, I am to believe that the Lord will help me? No: it is not so, although it often is so understood.

In a conflict it is of supreme importance that I should be in a stronghold or fortress which cannot be taken. With such a stronghold a weak garrison can offer resistance to a powerful enemy. Our conflict as Christians is now no longer concerned with going into the fortress. No: we have gone in, and are now in; and so long as we remain in it, we are invincible. The stronghold, this stable fort, is Christ. (Ps. 18:3; 46:2; 62:2,3,6,7,8; 144:2; Eph. 6:10) By faith we are in Him: by faith we know that the enemy can make no progress against our fortress. The wiles of Satan all go forth on the line of enticing us out of our fortress, of engaging us in conflict with him on the open plain. There he always overcomes. But if we only strive in faith, abiding in Christ by faith, then we overcome, because Satan then has to deal with Him, and because He then fights and overcomes. (Ex. 14:14; Josh 5:14; 2 Chron. 23:15; John 26:33; Rom. 8:37; 2 Cor. 2:14) This is the victory that hath overcome the world, even our faith.' Our first and greatest work is thus to believe. As Paul said before he mentions the warlike equipment of the Christian: From henceforth be strong in the Lord, and in the strength of His might.'

The reason why the victory is only by faith, and why the fight of faith is the good fight, is this: it is the Lord Jesus who purchased the victory, and who therefore alone gives power and dominion over the enemy. If we are, and abide, in Him, and surrender ourselves to live in Him, and by faith appropriate what He is, then the victory is in itself our own. We then understand: The battle is not yours, but God's. The Lord your God shall fight for you, and ye shall be still.' Just as we in opposition to God can achieve nothing good of ourselves, but in Christ please Him, so also is it in opposition to Satan: in ourselves we achieve nothing, but in Christ we are more than conquerors. By faith we stand in Him righteous before God, and just so in Him are we strong against our enemies. (Ps. 44:4,9; Isa. 45:24)

In this light we can read and take home to ourselves all the noble passages in the Old Testament, especially in the Psalms, where the glorious conflict of God in behalf of his people is spoken of. Fear, or spiritlessness, or uncertainty, makes weak, and cannot overcome: faith in the living God is equal to everything. (Deut. 20:3,8; Josh. 6:20; Judges 7:3 Ps. 18:32-40; Heb. 11:23) In Christ this truth is now still more real. God has come near. His power works in us who believe; it is really He that fights for us.

O Lord Jesus, who art the Prince of the army of the Lord, the Hero,the Victor, teach me to be strong in Thee my stronghold, and in thepower of Thy might. Teach me to understand what the good fight offaith is, and how the one thing that I have need of is, always tolook to Thee, to Thee, the supreme Guide of faith. And,consequently, in me, too, let this be the victory that overcomeththe world, namely, my faith. Amen.

1. The conflict of faith is no civil war, in which one half of the kingdom is divided against the other. This would be insurrection. This is the one conflict that many Christians know: the unrest of the conscience, and the powerless wrestling of a will which consents

to that which is good, but does not perform it. The Christian has not to overcome himself. This his Lord does when he surrenders himself. Then he is free and strong to combat and overcome the enemies of his Lord and of the kingdom. No sooner, however, are we willing that God should have His way with us than we are found striving against God. This also is truly conflict, but it is not the good fight of faith.

2. In Galatians 5 reference is made to the inner conflict; for the Galatians had not yet entirely surrendered themselves to the Spirit, to walk after the Spirit. The connection,' says Lange, shows that this conflict betwixt the flesh and the Spirit of God is not endless, but that there is expected of the Christian a complete surrender of himself, in order to be led only by the one principle—the Spirit; and then, further, a refusal to obey the flesh.' The believer must not strive against the flesh, to overcome it: this he cannot do. What he is to do is to choose to whom he will subject himself: by the surrender of faith to Christ, to strive in Him through the Spirit, He has a divine power for overcoming.

3. Hence, as we have seen in connection with the beginning of the new life, our one work every day and the whole day is to believe. Out of faith come all blessings and powers, also the victory for overcoming.

29. Be A Blessing

Get thee out of they country, and from thy kindred, and from thy father's house, unto the land that I will show thee; and I will make of thee a great nation, and I will bless thee; and be thou a blessing.'—Gen. 12:1,2

In these first words that God spake to Abraham, we have the short summary of all that God has to say to him and to us as His children. We see what the goal is to which God calls us, what the power that carries us to that goal, and what the place where the power is found.

Be a blessing: that is the goal for which God separates Abraham and every believing child of His.

God would have him and us made to understand that, when he blesses us, this is certainly not simply to make us happy, but that we should still further communicate His blessing. (Matt. 5:34,35; 10:8; 18:33) God Himself is love, and therefore He blesses. Love seeketh not itself: when the love of God comes to us, it will seek others through us. (Isa. 43:10,11; 1 Cor. 13:5; 1 John 4:11) The young Christian must from the beginning understand that he has received grace with the definite aim of becoming a blessing to others. Pray, keep not for yourself what the Lord gives to you for others. Offer yourself expressly and completely to the Lord, to be used by Him for others: that is the way to be blessed oveflowingly yourself. (Ps. 112:5,9; Prov. 11:24,25; Matt. 25:40; 1 Cor. 15;58;

2 Cor. 9:6; Heb. 6:10)

The power for this work will be given. Be a blessing': I will bless thee,' says the Lord. You are to be personally blessed yourself, personally sanctified and filled with the Spirit, and peace, and power of the Lord: then you have power to bless. (Luke 24:49; John 7:38; 14:12) In Christ God has blessed us with all spiritual things': let Jesus fill you with these blessings, and you shall certainly be a blessing: you need not doubt or fear. The blessing of God includes in it the power of life for multiplication, for expansion, for communication. See in the Scriptures how blessing and multiplication go together. (Gen. 1:22,28; 9:1; 22:17; 26:24) Blessing always includes the power to bless others. Only give the word of the Almighty God, I will bless Thee,' time to sink into your spirit. Wait upon God, that He Himself may say to you, I will bless thee.' Let your faith cleave fast to this. God will make it truth to you above all asking and thinking. (2 Cor. 9:8,11; Eph. 1:3; Heb. 6:14)

But for this end you must also betake yourself to the place of blessing: the land of promise, the simple life of faith in the promises. Get thee out thy land and thy father's house,' says the Lord. Departure, separation from the life of nature and the flesh, in which we were born of our father Adam, is what God would have. The offering up of what is most precious to man is the way to the blessing of God. (Luke 28:29,30; John 12:24,25; 2 Cor. 6:17,18) Get thee to a land that I will show thee,' says the Lord, out of the old life to a new life, where I alone am your guide; that is, a life where God can have me wholly for Himself alone, where I walk only on the promises of God—a life of faith.

Christian, God will in a Divine fashion fulfil to you His promise, I will bless thee.' O go, pray, out of your land and your father's house, out of the life of nature and the flesh, out of intercourse with the flesh and this world, to the New Life, the life of the Spirit, the life in fellowship with God to which He will lead you. There you become receptive of His blessing; there your heart becomes open to full faith in His word, I will bless thee'; there He can fulfil that word to you, and make you full of His blessing and power to be a blessing to others. Live with God, separated from the world: then shall you hear the voice of God speak with power: I will bless thee'; Be thou a blessing.'

O my Father, show me the way to that promised land where Thoubringest Thy people to have them wholly for Thyself. I will abandoneverything to follow Thee, to hold converse with Thee alone, inorder that Thou mayest fill me with Thy blessing. Lord, let Thyword, I will bless thee,' live in my heart as a word of God: thenshall I give myself wholly to live for others and to be a blessing.Amen.

1. God is the great, the only Fountain of blessing: as much of God as I have in me, so much blessing can I bring. I can work much for others without blessing. Actually to be a blessing, I must begin with that word, I will bless thee': then the other, Be a blessing' becomes easy.

2. In order to become a blessing, begin on a small scale: yield yourself up for others. Live to make others happy. Believe that the love of God dwells in you by the Spirit, and give yourself wholly to be a blessing and a joy to those who are round about you. Pray God to shed abroad His love in you still further by the Spirit. And believe very firmly that God can make you a greater blessing than you can think, if you surrender yourself to Him for this end.

3. But this surrender must have time in solitary prayer, that God may obtain possession of your spirit. This is for you the departure from your father's house: separate yourself from men that God may speak with you.

4. What think you? Was Abraham ever filled with regret that he placed himself so entirely under the leading of God? Then do you likewise.

5. Do you now know the two words which are the source of all promises and all commands to the children of believing Abraham? The promise is: I will bless thee.' The command is: Be a blessing.' Pray, take them both firmly for yourself.

6. And do you now understand where these two words to Abraham are fulfilled? In separation from his father's house—in the walk in fellowship with God.

30. Personal Work

Restore unto me the joy of Thy salvation: and uphold me with a free spirit. Then will I teach transgressors Thy ways; and sinners shall be converted unto Thee.'—Ps. 51:12,13

I believe, for I will speak.'—Ps. 116:10

But ye shall receive power, when the Holy Ghost is come upon you.'—Acts. 1:8

Every redeemed man is called to be a witness for his Lord. Not only by a godly walk, but by personal effort must I serve and make known my Lord. My tongue, my speech, is one of the principal means of intercourse with others and influence upon them. It is but a half dedication, when I do not also bring the offering of the lips, to speak for the Lord. (Ps. 40:10,11; 66:16; 71:8,15,24; Heb 13:15)

Of this work there is inconceivably real need. There are thousands of Christians who continually enjoy the preaching of the word, and yet do not understand the way of salvation. The Lord Jesus not only preached to the multitudes, but also spoke to individuals according to their needs. (Luke 7:40; John 3:3; 4:7) Scripture is full of examples of those who told to others what the Lord had done for them, and who thus became a blessing to them. (Ex. 18:8,1; 2 Chron. 5:3) The teacher alone cannot do this work of personal speaking: every ransomed soul must co-operate with him.He is in the world as a witness for his Lord. His own life cannot come to its full healthy increase, if he does not confess his Lord and work for Him.

That witness for the Lord must be a personal witness. We must have the courage to say, He has redeemed me: He will also redeem you: will you not accept this redemption? Come, let me show you the way.' (John 1:42,46; 4:28,39; Acts. 11:19) There are hundreds who would be glad if the personal question were put to them, Are you redeemed? What keeps you back? Can I not help you to go to the Lord?' Parents ought to speak personally with their children, and put the question, My child, have you already received the Lord

Jesus?' Teachers in Sabbath schools and in day schools, when they teach the word of God, ought to bring forward the personal question, whether the children have really received salvation, and ought to seek the opportunity of also putting the question to them separately. Friends must speak with their friends. Yes: before all else should this work be done.

Such work must be the work of love. Let souls feel that you love them tenderly. Let the humility and gentleness of love, as this was to be seen in Jesus, be seen also in you. At every turn surrender yourself to Jesus to be filled with His love: not by feeling, but by faith in this love, can you do your work. Beloved, keep yourselves in the love of God. And on some have mercy who are in doubt; and some save, snatching them out of the fire; and on some have mercy with fear.' The flesh often thinks that strength and force do more than love and patience. But that is not so: love achieves everything: it has overcome on the cross. (Heb. 3:13; 10:24; Jude 21:23)

Such work must be the work of faith, of faith working by love: faith that the Lord desires to use you and will use you. Be not afraid on account of your weakness: learn in the Scriptures what glorious promises God from time to time gave to those who had to speak for Him. (Ex. 4:11,12; Josh. 1:9;Isa. 50:4,11; Jer. 1:6,7; Matt. 10:19,20) Surrender yourself continually to God to be used for the rescue of souls, and take your stand on the fact that He who has redeemed you for this end, will for this end bless you. Although your work is in weakness and fear, although no blessing appears to come, be of good courage: at His time, we shall reap. (2 Chron. 15:7; Ps. 126:6,7; Hag. 2:5; Gal. 8:9; 1 John 5:16) Be filled with faith in the power of God, in His blessing upon you, and in the certainty of the hearing of prayer. If any man see his brother sinning a sin not unto death, he shall ask, and God will give him life.' Whether it be the most miserable and neglected, or whether it be the decent but indifferent who does not know his sin, take courage, the Lord is mighty to bless: He hears prayer.

But above all,—for this is the principal point,—carry out this work in fellowship with Jesus. Live closely with Him—live entirely for Him—let Jesus be in all your own life and He will speak and work in you. (Acts. 4:13; 2 Cor. 3:5; 8:3) Be full of the blessing of the Lord, full of His Spirit and His love, and it cannot be otherwise than that you should be a blessing. You shall be able to tell what He is continually for you. You shall have the love and the courage, with all humility, to put to souls the question, Is it well with you? Have you indeed the Lord Jesus as your Saviour?' And the Lord will made you experience the rich blessing which is promised to those who live to bless others.

Young Christian, be a witness for Jesus. Live as one who is wholly given away to Him to watch and to work for His honour.

Blessed Lord, who hast redeemed me to serve the Father in theproclamation of His love, I will with a free spirit offer myself toThee for this end. Fill my heart for this end with love to Him, toThee, and to souls. Cause me to see what an honour it is to do thework of redeeming love, even as Thou didst do it. Strengthen myconfidence that Thou art working with Thy power in my weakness. Andlet my joy be to help souls to Thee. Amen.

1. The question is often asked, What can I do to work for the Lord? Can you not take a class in the Sabbath school? Perhaps you live in the country where there are children that have no hour of the Sabbath devoted to them. Perhaps there are heathen children, or even grown-up people of the farms, who do not go to Church. See whether you cannot gather them together in the name of Jesus. Make it a matter of prayer and faith. Although you do this work with trembling, you may be sure that to begin to work will make you strong.

Or can you do nothing for the circulation of books and tracts? When you have a book that has been useful to you, order six or twelve copies of it. Speak of it, and offer it for sale: you can do great service by this means. So also with tracts: if you are too poor to give them for nothing, have them to sell: you may procure blessing by this method. It will especially help you to speak to others, if you begin with telling what is in a book.

2. But the principal thing is personal speaking. Do not hold back because you feel no freedom. The Lord will give you freedom in His own time. It is incredible how many are lost through ignorance. No one has ever personally made it clear to them how they can be saved. The thought that a change must first be sought and felt is so deeply rooted that the most faithful preaching is often of no avail against it. By their erroneous ideas, people misunderstand everything. Begin then to speak and to help souls to understand that they are to receive Jesus just as they are, that they can certainly know that He receives them, and that this is the power of a new and holy life.

31. Missionary Work

And He said unto them, Go ye into all the world, and preach the gospel to the whole creation. And they went forth, and preached everywhere, the Lord working with them, and confirming the word by the signs that followed.'—Mark 16:15,20

Every friend of Jesus is a friend of missions. Where there is a healthy spiritual life, there is a love for the missionary cause. When you consider the reasons of this, you obtain an insight into the glory of missions, and into your calling to embrace this cause as apart of your soul's life. Come and hear how much there is to make missionary work glorious and precious.

1. It is the cause for which Jesus left the throne of heaven. The heathen are His inheritance, given to Him by His Father. It is in heathendom that the power of Satan has been established. Jesus must have Himself vindicated as the conqueror. His glory, the coming and manifestation of His kingdom, depend on missions. (Isa. 2:8; Matt. 24:14; 28:18,28; Mark 13:10; Luke 21:24; Rom. 11:25)

2. Missionary work is the principal aim of the church on earth. All the last words of the Lord Jesus teach us this. (Mark. 26:15; Luke 24:47; John 27:18; Acts 1:8) The Lord is the head and He has made himself dependent upon His body, upon His members, by whom alone He can do His work. (1 Cor. 7:21) As a member of Christ, as a member of the church, shall I not give myself to take

part in the work, that this goal may be reached?

3. It is the work for which the Holy Spirit was given. See this in the promise of the Spirit: in the leading of the Spirit vouschafed to Peter and Barnabas and Saul. (Acts 1:8; 11:12,23,24; 8:2,4; 22:21) In the history of the Church we find that times of revival go hand in hand with new zeal for the missionary cause. The Holy Spirit is always a holy enthusiasm for the extension of the kingdom.

4. Missionary work brings blessing on the Church. It rouses to heroic deeds of faith and self-denial. It has furnished the most glorious instances of the wondrous power of the Lord. It gives heavenly joy over the conversion of sinners to those who watch for it with love and prayer. It cleanses the heart to understand God's great plans, and to await the fulfilment of them in supplication. Missionary work is a token of life in a Church, and brings more life. (Acts 14:287; 15:4,5; Rom. 11:25,33; 15:10; Eph. 3:5,8,10)

5. What a blessing it is for the world. What would we have been, had not missionaries come to our heathen forefathers in Europe? What a glorious blessing has onto missionary work already won in some lands? What help is there for the hundred millions of heathen, if not in missions? (Isa. 49:6,12,18,22; 54:1,2) Heaven and hell look upon missions as the battlefield where the powers of Satan and of Jesus Christ encounter one another. Alas! that the conflict should be carried on so feebly.

6. There will be a blessing for your own soul in love for missionary work. (Prov. 11:24,25; Isa. 58:7,8)

You will be exercised in faith. Missionary work is a cause for faith, where everything goes on slowly, and not according to the fancy of men. You will learn to cleave to God and the word.

Love will be awakened. You will learn to go out of yourselves and your little circle, and with an open eye and a large heart to live in the interests of your Lord and King: you will feel how little true love you have, and you will receive more love.

You will be drawn into prayer. Your calling and power as an intercessor will become clearer to you, and therewith the blessedness of thus co-operation for the kingdom. You will discern how it is the highest conformity to Him who came to seek the lost, to give up your own ease and rest to fight in love the fight of prayer against Satan in behalf of the heathen.

Young Christian, missionary work is more glorious and holy than you suppose. There is more blessing in it than you are aware of. The new life in you depends upon it more than you can as yet understand. Yield yourself up anew in obedience to the word to give missions a large place in your heart; yes, in your heart. The Lord Himself will further teach and bless you.

And if you would know how to have your love for missions, as the work of your Lord, increased, attend to the following hints: - Become acquainted with the missionary cause. Endeavour by writings and books to know what the condition and need of heathendom is; what, by the blessing of the Lord, has been already done there; what the work is that is being done now. Speak with others about this cause. Perhaps there could be instituted in your neighbourhood a little missionary society. Perhaps one of your prayer-meetings, say, once a month, could be set apart for prayer in behalf of the missionary cause. Pray also for this in secret. Let the coming of the kingdom have a definite place in your secret prayers. Endeavour to follow the material for prayer in the promises of the word about the heathen, in the whole Scriptures, especially in the prophet Isaiah. (Isa. 49:6,18,21,22; 54:1,3; 60:1,3,11,16; 62:2) Give also for missions: not only when you are asked; not merely what you can spare without feeling it; but set apart for this cause a portion of what you possess or earn. Let the Lord see that you are in earnest with His work. If there is missionary work that is being done in your neighbourhood, show yourself a friend to it. Although there be much imperfection in that work,—and where is there work of man that is perfect?—complain not of the imperfection, but look upon the essence of the cause, the endeavour to obey the command of the Lord, and give your prayer and your help. A friend of Jesus is a friend of missions. Love for missionary work is an indispensable element of the new life.

Son of God, when Thou didst breathe Thy Spirit upon Thy disciples,saying, Receive ye the Holy Ghost,' Thou didst add: As the Fatherhath sent Me, even so send I you.' Lord, here am I: send me also.Breathe Thy Spirit into me also, that I may live for Thy kingdom.Amen.

1. Unknown makes unbeloved,' is a word that is specially true of missionary work. He who is acquainted with the wonders that God has wrought in some lands, will praise and thank God for what the missionary enterprise has achieved, and will be strengthened in his faith that missionary work is really God's own cause.

Among the books that help to awaken interest in missions are biographies of missionaries. The life of Henry Martyn' is one, formerly issued by the Book Society. Uncle Charles' is the name of a book with an account of missionary work in South Africa. Some books on missions are generally to be found in our Sabbath school libraries.

2. We should never forget that the missionary cause is an enterprise of faith. It requires faith in the promises of God, in the power of God. It has need of love—love to Jesus, whereby the heart is filled with desire for His honour, and love to souls, that longs for their safety. It is a work of the Spirit of God, whom the world cannot receive': therefore the world can approve of missions only when they go forward with the highest prosperity.

3. Let no friend of missions become discouraged when the work proceeds slowly. Although all baptized men are not converted, although even amongst the converts there is still much perversity, and some fall back after a fair professions. Amongst our forefathers in Europe, a whole century was occupied with the introduction of Christianity. Sometimes a nation received Christianity to cast it off

again after thirty or forty years. It required a thousand years to bring them up to the height at which we now stand. Let us not expect too much from the heathen at once, but with love and patience and firm faith, pray and work, and expect the blessing of God.

32. Light And Joyfulness

Blessed is the people that know the joyful sound: they walk, O Lord, in the light of Thy Continence. In Thy name do they rejoice all the day.'—Ps. 89:15,16

Light is sown for the righteous, and gladness for the upright in heart.'—Ps. 47:11

I am the Light of the world: he that followeth me shall not walk in the darkness, but shall have the light of life.'—John 8:12

I will see you again, and your heart shall rejoice, and your joy no one taketh away from you.'—John 16:22

As sorrowful, yet always rejoicing.'—2 Cor. 6:10

A father will always be eager to see his children joyful. He does all that he can to make them happy. Hence God also desires that His children should walk before Him in gladness of heart. He has promised them gladness: He will give it. (Ps. 89:16,17; Isa. 29:29; John 26:22; 1 Pet. 1:8) He has commanded it: we must take it and walk in it at all times. (Ps. 32:1; Isa. 12:5,6; 1 Thess. 5:16; Phil. 4:4)

The reason of this is not difficult to find. Gladness is always the token that something really satisfies me and has great value for me. More than anything else is gladness for what I possess a recommendation of it to others. And gladness in God is the strongest proof that I have in God what satisfies and satiates me, that I do not serve Him with dread, or to be kept, but because He is my salvation. Gladness is the token of the truth and the worth of obedience, showing whether I have pleasure in the will of God. (Deut. 28:47; Ps. 40:9; 119:11) It is for this reason that joy in God is so acceptable to Him, so strengthening to believers themselves, and to all who are around the most eloquent testimony of what we think of God. (Neh. 8:11; Ps. 68:4; Prov. 4:18)

In the Scriptures light and gladness are frequently connected with each other. (Esth. 8:16; Prov. 13:9; 15:30; Isa. 60:20) It is so in nature. The joyful light of the morning awakens the birds to their song and gladdens the watchers who in the darkness have longed for the day. It is the light of God's countenance that gives the Christian his gladness: in fellowship with his Lord, he can, and always will, be happy: the love of the Father shines like the sun upon His children. (Ex. 10:23; 2 Sam. 23:4; Ps. 36:10; Isa. 60:1,20; 1 John 1:5; 4:16) When darkness comes over the soul, it is always through one of two things, through sin or through unbelief. Sin is darkness, and makes dark. And unbelief also makes dark, for it turns us from Him, who alone is the light.

The question is sometimes put, Can the Christian walk always in the light? The answer of our Lord is clear, He that followeth Me shall not walk in darkness.' It is sin, the turning from behind Jesus to our own way, that makes dark. But at the moment we confess sin, and have it cleansed in the blood, we are again in the light. (Josh. 7:13; Isa. 58:10; 59:1,2,9; Matt. 15:14,15; 2 Cor. 6:14; Eph. 5:8,14; 1 Thess. 5:5; 1 John 2:10) Or it is unbelief that makes dark. We look to ourselves and our strength; we would seek comfort in our own feeling, or our own works, and all becomes dark. As soon as we look to Jesus, to the fulness, to the perfect provision for our needs that is in Him, all is light. He says, I am the Light: he that followeth me shall not walk in darkness, but shall have the light of life.' So long as I believe, I have light and gladness. (John 12:36; 11:40; Rom. 15:13; 1 Pet. 1:8)

Christians, who would walk according to the will of the Lord, hear what His word says: Finally, my brethren, rejoice in the Lord. Rejoice in the Lord always: again, I will say, Rejoice.' (Phil. 3:1; 4:3) In the Lord Jesus there is joy unspeakable, and full of glory: believing in Him, rejoice in this. Live the life of faith: that life is salvation and glorious joy. A heart that gives itself undividedly to follow Jesus, that lives by faith in Him and His love, shall have light and gladness. Therefore, soul, only believe. Do not seek gladness; in that case you will not find it, because you are seeking feeling. But seek Jesus, follow Jesus, believe in Jesus, and gladness shall be added to you. Not seeing, but believing, rejoice with joy unspeakable and full of glory.'

Lord Jesus, Thou are the Light of the world, the Effulgence of theunapproachable light, in whom we see the light of God. From Thycountenance radiates upon us the illumination of the knowledge ofthe love and glory of God. And thou art ours, our light and oursalvation. O teach us to believe more firmly that with Thee we cannever walk in the darkness. Let gladness in Thee be the proof thatThou art all to us, and our strength to do all that Thou wouldsthave us do. Amen.

1. The gladness that I have in anything is the measure of its worth in my eyes: the gladness in a person, the measure of my pleasure in him: the gladness in a work the measure of my pleasure in it. Gladness in God and His service is one of the surest tokens of healthy spiritual life.

2. Gladness is hindered by ignorance, when we do not rightly understand God and His love and the blessedness of His service: by unbelief, when we still seek something in our own strength or feeling: by double-heartedness, when we are not willing to give up and lay aside everything for Jesus.

3. Understand this saying: He that seeks gladness shall not find it; he that seeks the Lord and His will, shall find gladness unsought.' Think over this. He that seeks gladness as a thing of

feeling, seeks himself: he would fain be happy: he will not find it. He that forgets himself to live in the Lord and His will, shall be taught of himself to rejoice in the Lord. It is God, God Himself, who is the God of the gladness of our rejoicing: seek God, and you have gladness. You have then simply to take and enjoy it by faith.

4. To thank much for what God is and does, to believe much in what God says and will do, is the way to abiding gladness.

5. The light of the eyes gladdens the heart.' God has not intended that His children should walk in the darkness. Satan is the prince of the darkness: God is light: Christ is the Light of the world: we are children of the light: let us walk in the light. Let us believe in the promise, The Lord shall be to thee an everlasting light. Thy sun shall no more go down, for the Lord shall be to thee an everlasting light, and the days of thy mourning shall be ended.

33. Chastisement

'Blessed is the man whom Thou chastenest, O Lord, and teachest out of Thy law; that Thou mayest give him rest from the days of adversity.'—Ps. 94:12

'Before I was afflicted, I went astray; but now I observe Thy word. It is good for me that I have been afflicted; that I might learn Thy statutes.'—Ps. 119:67,71

'He chastens us for our profit, that we may be partakers of His holiness.'—Heb. 12:10

'Count it all joy, my brethren, when ye fall into manifold temptations; knowing that the proof of your faith worketh patience.'—Jas. 1:2,3

Every child of God must at one time or another enter the school of trial. What the Scriptures teach us is confirmed by experience. And the Scriptures teach us further, that we are to count it a joy when God takes us into this school. It is a part of our heavenly blessedness to be educated and sanctified by the Father through chastisement.

Not that trial in itself brings a blessing. (Isa. 5:3; Hos. 7:14,15; 2 Cor. 7:10) Just as there is no profit in the ground's being made wet by rain or broken up by the plough, when no seed is cast into it, so there are children of God that enter into trial and have little blessing from it. The heart is softened for a time, but they know not how to obtain an abiding blessing from it. They know not what the Father has in view with them in the school of trial.

In a good school there are four things necessary—a definite aim, a good text-book, a capable teacher, a willing pupil.

1. Let the aim of trial be clear to you. Holiness is the highest glory of the Father, and also of the child. He chastens us for our profit that we may be partakers of His Holiness.' (Isa. 27:8,9; 1 Cor. 11:32; Heb. 2:10; 12:11) In trial the Christian would often have only comfort. Or he seeks to be quiet and contented under the special chastisement. This is indeed the beginning; but the Father desires something else, something higher. He would make him holy, holy, for his whole life. When Job said, Blessed be the name of the Lord,' this was still but the beginning of his school-time: the Lord had still more to teach him. God would unite our will with His holy will, not only on the one point in which He is trying us, but in everything: God would fill us with His holy Spirit, with His holiness. This is the aim of God; this also must be your aim in the school of trial.

2. Let the word of God at this time be your reading book. See in our trials how in affliction God would teach us out of His law. The word will reveal to you why the Father chastens you, how deeply He loves you in the midst of it, and how rich are the promises of His consolation. Trial will give new glory to the promises of the Father. In chastisement have recourse to the word. (Ps. 119:49,50,92,143; Isa. 40:1; 43:2; 1 Thess. 4:8)

3. Let Jesus be your teacher. He Himself was sanctified by suffering: it was in suffering that He learned full obedience. He has a wonderfully sympathetic heart. Have much intercourse with Him. Seek not your comfort from much speaking on the part of men or with men. Give Jesus the opportunity of teaching you. Have much converse with Him in solitude. (Isa. 26:16; 61:1,2; Heb. 2:10,17,18; 5:9) The Father has given you the word, the Spirit, the Lord Jesus your sanctification, in order to sanctify you: affliction and chastisement are meant to bring you to the word, to

Jesus Himself, in order that He may make you partaker of His holiness. It is in fellowship with Jesus that consolation comes as of itself (2 Cor. 1:3,4; Heb. 13:5,6)

4. Be a willing pupil. Acknowledge your ignorance. Think not that you understand the will of God. Ask and expect that the Lord would teach you the lesson that you are to learn in affliction. To the meek there is the promise of teaching and wisdom. Seek to have the ear open, the heart very quiet, and turned towards God. Know that it is the Father that has placed you in the school of trial: yield yourself with all willingness to hear you taught. He will bless you greatly in this. (Ps. 25:9;39:2,10; Isa. 50:4,5)

Happy is the man whom Thou chastenest, and teachest out of Thy law.' Count it all joy when ye fall into manifold temptations,' that ye may be perfect, lacking in nothing.' Regard the time of trial as a time of blessing, as a time of close converse with the Father, of being made partaker of His holiness, and you shall also rejoicingly say: It is good for me that I have been afflicted.'

Father, what thanks shall I express to Thee for the glorious lightthat Thy word casts upon the dark trials of this life. Thou wilt bythis means teach me, and make me partaker of Thy holiness. HastThou considered the suffering and the death of Thy beloved Son nottoo much to bring holiness near to me, and shall I not be willing toendure Thy chastisement to be partaker of it? No: Father, thanks beunto Thee for Thy precious work: only fulfil Thy counsel in me.Amen.

1. In chastisement it is first of all necessary that we should be possessed by the thought: This is the will of God. Although the trial comes through our own folly or the perversity of men, we must acknowledge that it is the will of God that we should be in that suffering by means of that folly or perversity. We see this clearly in Joseph and the Lord Jesus. Nothing will give us rest but the willing acknowledgment: this is the will of God.

2. The second thought is: God wills not only the trial, but also the consolation, the power, and the blessing in it. He who acknowledges the will of God in the chastisement itself is on the way to see and experience the accompaniments also as the will of God.

3. The will of God is as perfect as He Himself: let us not be afraid to surrender ourselves to it: no one suffers loss by deeming the will of God unconditionally good.

4. This is holiness: to know and to adore the will of God, to unite one's self wholly with it.

5. Pray, seek not comfort in trial in connection with men. Do not mingle too much with them: see to it rather that you deal with God and His word. The object of trial is just to draw you away from what is earthly, in order that you may turn to God and give Him time to unite your will with His perfect will.

34. Prayer

Thou, when thou prayest, enter into thine inner chamber, and having shut the door, pray to thy Father which is in secret, and thy Father which seeth in secret shall recompense thee.' —Matt. 6:6

The spiritual life with its growth depends in great measure on prayer. According as I pray much or little, pray with pleasure or as a duty, pray according to the word of God or my own inclination, will my life flourish or decay. In the word of Jesus quoted above, we have the leading ideas of true prayer.

Alone with God: that is the first thought. The door must be shut, with the world and man outside, because I am to have converse with God undisturbed. When God met with His servants in the olden time, He took them alone. (Gen. 28:22,23; 22:5; 32:24; Ex. 33:11) Let the first thought in your prayer be: here are God and I in the chamber with each other. According to your conviction of the nearness of God will be the power of your prayer.

In the presence of your Father: this is the second thought. You come to the inner chamber, because your Father with His love awaits you there. Although you are cold, dark, sinful; although it is doubtful whether you can pray at all; come, because the Father is there, and there looks upon you. Set yourself beneath the light of his eye. Believe in His tender fatherly love, and out of this faith prayer will be born. (Matt. 6:8; 7:11)

Count certainly upon an answer: that is the third point in the word of Jesus. Your Father will recompense you openly.' There is nothing about which the Lord Jesus has spoken so positively as the certainty of an answer to prayer. Pray, review the promises. (Matt 6:7,8; 11:24; Luke 28:8; John 14:13,14; 15:7,16; 16:23,24) Observe how constantly in the Psalms, that prayer-book of God's saints, God is called upon as the God who hears prayer and gives answers. (Ps. 3:5; 4:4; 6:10; 10:17; 27:6,22,25; 20:2,7,10; 34:5,7,18; 38:16; 40:2; 65:3; 66:19)

It may be that there is much in you that prevents the answer. Delay in the answer is a very blessed discipline. It leads to self-searching as to whether we are praying amiss, and whether our life is truly in harmony with our prayer. It rouses to a purer exercise of faith. (Josh. 7:12; 1 Sam. 8:18; 14:37,38; 28:6,15; Prov. 21:13; Isa. 1:15; Mic. 3:4; Hag. 1:9; Jas. 1:6; 4:3; 5:16) It conducts to a closer and more persistent converse with God. The sure confidence of an answer is the secret of powerful praying. Let this always be with us the chief thing in prayer. When you pray, stop in the midst of your prayer to ask, Do I believe that I am receiving what I pray for? Let your faith receive and hold fast the answer as given: it shall turn out according to your faith. (Ps. 145:9; Isa. 30:19; Jer. 33:3; Mal. 3:10; Matt. 9:29; 15:28; 1 John 3:22; 5:14,15)

Beloved young Christians, if there is one thing about which you must be conscientious, it is this: secret converse with God. Your life is hid with Christ in God. Every day must you in prayer ask from above, and by faith receive in prayer what you need for that day. Every day must personal intercourse with the Father and the Lord Jesus be renewed and strengthened. God is our salvation and our strength: Christ is our life and our holiness: only in personal fellowship with the living God is our blessedness found.

Christian, pray much, pray continually, pray without ceasing. When you have no desire to pray, go just then to the inner chamber. Go as one who has nothing to bring to the Father, to set yourself before Him in faith in His love. That coming to the Father, and abiding before Him, is already a prayer that He understands. Be assured that to appear before God, however passively, always brings a blessing. The Father not only hears: He sees in secret, and He will recompense it openly.

O my Father, who hast so certainly promised in Thy word to hear theprayer of faith, give to me the Spirit of prayer, that I may knowhow to offer that prayer. Graciously reveal to me Thy wonderfulFatherly love, the complete blotting out of my sins in Christ, bywhich every hindrance in this direction is taken away, and theintercession of the Spirit in me, by which my ignorance or weaknesscannot deprive me of the blessing. Teach me with faith in Thee, theThree-One, to pray in fellowship with Thee. And confirm me in thestrong living certitude that I receive what I believingly ask.Amen.

1. In prayer the principal thing is faith. The whole of salvation, the whole of the new life is by faith, therefore also by prayer. There is all too much prayer that brings nothing, because there is little faith in it. Before I pray, and while I pray, and after I have prayed, I must ask: Do I pray in faith? I must say: I believe with my whole heart.

2. To arrive at this faith we must take time in prayer: time to set ourselves silently and trustfully before God, and to become awake to His presence: time to have our soul sanctified in fellowship with God: time for the Holy Spirit to teach us to hold fast and use trustfully the word of promise. No earthly knowledge, no earthly possessions, no earthly food, no intercourse with friends, can we have without time, sufficient time. Let us not think to learn how to pray, how to enjoy the power and the blessedness of prayer, if we do not take time with God.

3. And then there must be not only time every day, but perseverance from day to day. Time is required to grow in the certitude that we are acceptable to the Father, and that our prayer has power, in the confidence which knows that our prayer is according to His will and is heard. We must not suppose that we know well enough how to pray, and can but ask, and then it is over.

No: prayer is converse and fellowship with God, in which God has time and opportunity to work in us, in which our souls die to their own will and power, and become bound up and united with God.

4. For encouragement in persistent prayer, the following instance may be of service. In an address delivered at Calcutta, George Muller recently said that in 1844 five persons were laid upon his heart, and that he began to pray for their conversion. Eighteen months passed by before the first was converted. He prayed five years more, when the second was converted. After twelve years and a half, yet another was converted. And now he also already prayed forty years for the other two, without letting slip a single day; and still they are not converted. He was, nevertheless, full of courage in the sure confidence that these two also would be given him in answer to his prayer.

35. The Prayer Meeting

Again I say unto you, that if two of you shall agree on earth as touching anything that they shall ask, it shall be done for them of My Father which is in heaven. For where two or three are gathered together in My name, there am I in the midst of them.'—Matt. 28:19,20

The Lord Jesus has told us to go into the inner chamber and hold our personal converse with God by prayer in secret, and not to be seen of men. The very same voice tells us that we are also to pray in fellowship with one another. (Matt. 6:6; Luke 9:18,28) And when He went to heaven, the birth of the Christian Church took place in a prayer meeting which one hundred and twenty men and women held for ten days. (Acts. 1:14) The Day of Pentecost was the fruit of unanimous persevering prayer. Let every one who would please the Lord Jesus, who desires the gift of the Spirit with power for his congregation or Church, who would have the blessing of fellowship with the children of God, attached himself to a prayer meeting, and prove the Lord whether He will make good His word and bestow upon it a special blessing. (2 Chron. 20:4,17; Neh. 9:2,3; Joel 2:16,17; Acts. 12:5) And let him give help in it, so that the prayer meeting may be such as the Lord presented it to us.

For a blessed prayer-meeting, there must be, first of all, agreement concerning the thing which we desire. There must be something that we really desire to have from God; and concerning this we are to be in harmony. There must be inner love and unity amongst the suppliants,—all that is strife, envy, wrath, lovelessness, makes prayer powerless, (Ps. 133:1,3; Jer. 58:4; Matt. 5:23,24; Mark. 11:25)—and then agreement on the definite object that is desired. (Jer. 32:39; Acts. 4:24) For this end it is entirely proper that what people are to pray for should be stated in the prayer meeting. Whether it be that one of the members would have his particular needs brought forward, or whether others would bring more general needs to the Lord, such as the conversion of the unconverted, the revival of God's children, the anointing of the teacher, the extension of the kingdom, let the objects be announced beforehand. And let no one then suppose that there is unanimity whenever one is content to join in prayer for these objects. No: we are to take them into our heart and life, bring them continually before the Lord, be inwardly eager that the Lord should give them: then we are on the way to the prayer that has power.

The second feature that characterizes a right prayer meeting is the coming together in the name of Jesus and the consciousness of His presence. The Scripture says, The name of the Lord is a strong tower: the righteous runneth into it, and is safe.' (Prov. 18:10) [4] The name is the expression of the person. When they come together, believers are to enter into the name of Jesus, to betake themselves within this name as their fortress and abode. In this name they mingle with one another before the Father, and out of this name they pray: this name makes them also truly one with each other. And when they are thus in this name, the living Lord Himself is in their midst: and He says that this is the reason why the Father certainly hears them. (John 14:13,14; 15:7,16; 16:23,24) They are in Him, and He is in them, and out of Him they pray, and their prayer comes before the Father in His power. O let the name of Jesus be really the point of union, the meeting place, in our prayer meetings, and we shall be conscious that He is in our midst.

Then there is the third feature of united prayer of which the Lord has told us: our request shall certainly be done of the Heavenly Father. The prayer shall certainly be answered. O we may well cry out in these days, Where is the God of Elijah?' for He was a God that answered. The God that shall answer, He shall be God,' said Elijah to the people. And he said to God, Answer me, Lord; answer me; that this people may acknowledge that Thou, O Lord, art God.' (1 Chron. 18:24,37; Jas. 5:16) When we are content with much praying, with continuous praying, without answer, then there will be little answer given. But when we understand that the answer as the token of God's pleasure in our prayer is the principal thing, and are not willing to be content without it, we shall discover what is lacking in our prayer, and shall set ourselves so to pray that an answer may come. And this surely we may firmly believe: the Lord takes delight in answering. It is a joy to Him when His people so enter into the name of Jesus, and pray out of it, that He can give what they desire. (Acts. 12:5; 2 Cor. 1:11; Jas. 4:8; 5:16,17)

Children of God, however young and weak you may still be, here is one of the institutions prepared for you by the Lord Jesus Himself to supply you with help in prayer. Let every one make use of the prayer meeting. Let every one go in a praying and believing frame of mind, seeking the name and the presence of the Lord. Let every one seek to live and pray with his brethren and sisters. And let every one expect surely to see glorious answers to prayer.

Blessed Lord Jesus, who hast given us commandment to pray, as wellin the solitary inner chamber as in public fellowship with oneanother, let the one habit always make the other more precious ascomplement and confirmation. Let the inner chamber prepare us, andawaken the need for union with Thy people in prayer. Let Thypresence there be our blessedness. And let fellowship with Thypeople strengthen us surely to expect and receive answers. Amen.

1. There are many places of our country where prayer meetings might be a great blessing. A pious man or woman who should once a week or on Sabbath at mid-day gather together the inhabitants on a farm-place or the neighbours of two or three places that are not far from one another, might be able to obtain great blessing. Let every believing reader of this portion inquire if there does not exist in his neighbourhood some such need, and let him make a beginning in the name of the Lord. Let me therefore earnestly put the question to every reader: Is there a prayer-meeting in your district? Do you faithfully take part in it? Do you know what it is to come together with the children of God in the name of Jesus, to experience His presence and His hearing of prayer?

2. There is a book, 'The Hour of Prayer,' with suitable portions for reading out in such gatherings. Or let this book, 'The New Life,' be taken, a portion read, and some of the texts reviewed and spoken upon: this will give material for prayer.

3. 'Will the prayer meeting do no harm to the inner chamber?' is a question sometimes asked. My experience is just the reverse of this result. The prayer meeting is a school of prayer. The weak learn from more advanced petitioners. Material for prayer is given: opportunity for self-searching; encouragement to more prayer.

4. Would that it were more general in prayer meetings for people to speak of definite objects for which to pray; things in which one can definitely and trustfully look out for an answer, and concerning which one can know when an answer comes. Such announcements would greatly further unanimity and believing expectations.

[4] The Dutch version has—'and is set in a high room.'—Translator

36. The Fear Of The Lord

Blessed is the man that feareth the Lord. He shall not be afraid of evil tidings. His heart is established, he shall not be afraid.'—Ps. 112:1,7,8

So the Church, walking in the fear of the Lord and in the comfort of the Holy Ghost, was multiplied.'—Acts 9:31

The Scriptures use the word fear' in a twofold way. In some places it speaks of fear' as something wrong and sinful, and in the strongest terms it forbids us to fear.' (Gen. 15:1; Isa. 8:13; Jer. 32:40; Rom. 8:15; 1 Pet. 3:14; 1 John 4:18) In well-nigh one hundred places occurs the word: Fear not.' In many other places, on the contrary, fear is praised as one of the surest tokens of true godliness, acceptable to the Lord, and fruitful of blessing to us. (Ps. 22:24,26; 33:18; 112:1; 115:13; Prov. 28:14) The people of God bear the name: those that fear the Lord. The distinction betwixt these two lies in this simple fact: the one is unbelieving fear, the other is believing. Where fear is found connected with lack of trust in God, there it is sinful and very hurtful. (Matt. 8:26; Rev. 21:9) The fear, on the other hand, that is coupled with trust and hope in God, is for the spiritual life entirely indispensable. The fear that has man and what is temporal for its object, is condemned. The fear that with childlike confidence and love honours the Father, is commanded. (Ps. 33:18; 147:11; Luke 12:4,7) It is the believing, not slavish, but filial, fear of the Lord that is presented by the

Scriptures as a source of blessing and power. He that fears the Lord will fear nothing else. The fear of the Lord will be the beginning of all wisdom. The fear of the Lord is the sure way to the enjoyment of God's favour and protection. (Ps. 56:5,12; Prov. 1:7; 9:10; 10:27; 19:23; Acts. 9:31; 2 Cor. 7:1)

There are some Christians who by their upbringing are led into the fear of the Lord, even before they come to faith. This is a very great blessing: parents can give a child no greater blessing than to bring him up in the fear of the Lord. When those who are thus brought up are brought to faith, they have a great advantage: they are, as it were, prepared to walk in the joy of the Lord. When, on the contrary, others that have not this preparation, come to conversion, they have need of special teaching and vigilance, in order to pray for and awaken this holy fear.

The elements of which this fear is composed are many and glorious. The principal are the following:—

There are holy reverence and awe before the glorious majesty of God and before the All Holy. These guard against the superficiality that forgets who God is, and that takes no pains to honour Him as God. (Job 42:6; Ps. 5:8; Isa. 6:2,5; Hab. 2:20; Zech. 2:3)

There is deep humility that is afraid of itself, and couples deep confidence in God with an entire distrust in itself. Conscious weakness that knows the subtlety of its own heart always dreads doing anything contrary to the will or honour of God. But just because he fears God, such an one firmly reckons on Him for protection. And this same humility inspires him in all his intercourse with his fellow-men. (Luke 18:2,4; Rom. 11:20; 1 Pet. 3:5)

There is circumspectness or vigilance. With holy forethought, it seeks to know the right path, to watch against the enemy, and to be guarded against all lightness or hastiness in speech, resolve, and conduct. (Prov. 2:5,11; 8:12,13; 13:33; 16:6; Luke 1:74)

And there are also in it holy zeal and courage in watching and striving. The fear of displeasing the Lord by not conducting one's self in everything as His servant, incites to being faithful in that which is least. The fear of the Lord takes all other fear away, and gives inconceivable courage in the certitude of victory. (Deut. 6:2; Isa. 12:2)

And out of this fear is then born joy. Rejoice with trembling:' the fear of the Lord gives joy its depth and stability. Fear is the root, joy the fruit: the deeper the fear, the higher the joy. On this account it is said: Ye that fear the Lord praise Him;' Ye that fear the Lord, bless the Lord.' (Ps. 22:24; 135:20)

Young disciples of Christ, hear the voice of your Father, Fear the Lord, ye His saints.' Let deep fear of the Lord and dread of all that might displease or grieve Him, fill you. Then shall you never have any evil to fear. He that fears the Lord and seeks to do all that pleases Him, for him shall God also do all that he desires. The childlike believing fear of God will lead you into the love and joy of God, while slavish, unbelieving, cowardly fear is utterly cast out.

O my God, unite my heart for the fear of Thy name. May I always beamongst those that fear the Lord, that hope in His mercy. Amen.

1. What are some of the blessings of the fear of God? (Ps. 31:20; 115:13; 127:11; 145:19; Prov. 1, 7,8,13,14,27; Acts 10:35)

2. What are the reasons why we are to fear God? (Deut. 10:17,20,21; Josh. 4:24; 1 Sam. 12:24; Jer. 5:22; 10:6,7; Matt. 10:28; Rev. 15:4)

3. It is especially the knowledge of God in His greatness, power, and glory that will fill the soul with fear. But for this end, we must set ourselves silent before Him, and take time for our soul to come under the impression of His majesty.

4. He delivered me from all my fears.' Does this apply to every different sort of fear by which you are hindered? There is the fear of man (Isa. 41:12,13; Heb 13:16); the fear of heavy trial (Isa.

40:1,2); the fear of our own weakness (Isa. 41:10); fear for the work of God (1 Chron. 28:20); the fear of death (Ps. 23:4).

5. Do you now understand the word: Blessed is the man that fears the Lord. His heart is established, he shall not be afraid'?

37. Undivided Consecration

And Ittai answered, As the Lord liveth, surely in what place my lord the king shall be, whether for death or for life, even there also will thy servant be.'—2 Sam. 15:21

Whosoever he be of you that renounceth not all that he hath, he cannot be My disciple.'—Luke 14:33

Come ye out from among them, and be ye separate, saith the Lord, and touch no unclean thing; and I will receive you, and will be to you a Father.'—2 Cor. 6:17,18

Yea verily, and I count all things to be loss for Christ Jesus my Lord.'—Phil. 3:8

We have already said that surrender to the Lord is something that for the Christian always obtains newer and deeper significance. When this takes place, he comes to understand how this surrender involves nothing less than a complete and undivided consecration to live only, always, wholly for Jesus. as entirely as the temple was dedicated to the service of God alone, so that every one knew that it existed only for that purpose; as entirely as the offering on the altar could be used only according to the command of God, and no one had a right to dispose of one portion of it otherwise than God had said: so entirely do you belong to your Lord, and so undivided must your consecration to Him be. God continually reminded Israel that He had redeemed them to be His possession. (Ex. 19:4,5; Lev. 1:8,9; Deut. 7:6; Rom. 12:1; 1 Cor. 3:16,17) Let us see what this implies.

There is personal attachment to Jesus, and intercourse with Him in secret. He will be, He must be, the beloved, the desire, the joy of our souls. It is not, in the first instance, to the service of God, but to Jesus as our Friend and King, our Redeemer and God, that we are to be consecrated. (John 14:21; 15:14,15; 21:17; Gal. 2:10) It is only the spiritual impulse of a personal cordial love that can set us in a condition for a life of complete consecration. Continually did Jesus use the words: For My sake,' Follow Me,' My disciple'; He Himself must be the central point. (Matt. 10:32,33,37,38,40: Luke 14:26,27,33; 18:22) He gave Himself: to desire to have Him, to love, to depend on Him, is the characteristic of a disciple.

Then there is public confession. What has been given to any one, that he will have acknowledged by all as his property. His possessions are his glory. When the Lord Jesus manifests His great grace to a soul in redeeming it, He desires that the world should see and know it: He would be known and honoured as its proprietor. He desires that every one that belongs to Him should confess Him, and that it should come out that Jesus is King. (Ex. 33:16; Josh. 24:15; John 13:35) Apart from this public confession, the surrender is but a half-hearted one. As a part of this public confession, it is also required that we should join His people and acknowledge them as our people. The one new commandment that the Lord gave, the sure token by which all should recognize that we are His disciples, is brotherly love. Although the children of God in a locality are few, or despised, or full of imperfection, yet do you join them. Love them: hold intercourse with them. Attach yourself to them in prayer meetings and otherwise. Love them fervently: brotherly love has wonderful power to open the heart for the love and the indwelling of God. (Ruth 1:16; John 15:12; Rom. 7:5; 1 Cor. 12:2021; Eph. 4:14,16; 1 Pet. 1:22)

To complete consecration, there also belongs separation from sin and the world. Touch not the unclean thing. Know that the world is under the power of the Evil One. Ask not how much of it you can retain without being lost. Ask not always what is sin and what is lawful. Even of that which is lawful, the Christian must oftentimes make a willing renunciation, in order to be able to live wholly for his God. (1 Cor. 8:13; 9:25,27; 10:23;2 Cor. 6:16,17; 2 Tim. 2:4) Abstinence even from lawful things is often indispensable for the full imitation of the Lord Jesus. Live as one who is really separated for God and His holiness. He who renounces everything, who counts everything loss for Jesus' sake, shall even in this life receive an hundredfold. (Gen. 22:16,17; 2 Chron. 25:9; Luke 18:29; John 12:24,25; Phil. 3:8)

And what I separate from everything, I will use. Entire consecration has its eye upon making us useful and fit for God and His service. Let there not be with you the least doubt as to whether God has need of you, and will make you a great blessing. Only give yourself unreservedly into His hands. Present yourself to Him, that He may fill you with His blessing, His love, His Spirit: you shall be a blessing. (2 Tim. 2:21)

Let no one fear that this demand for a complete consecration is too high for him. You are not under the law which demands, but gives no power. You are under grace, which itself works what it requires. (2 Cor. 9:8; 2 Thess. 1:11,12) Like the first surrender, so is every fresh dedication yielded to this Jesus, whom the Father has given to do all things for you. Consecration is a deed of faith, a part of the glorious life of faith. It is on this account that you have to say: It is not I, but the grace of God in me, that will do it. I live only by faith in Him who works in me as well the willing as the performance. (1 Cor. 15:10; Gal. 2:20; Phil. 2:13)

Blessed Lord, open the eyes of my heart that I may see howcompletely Thou wouldst have me for Thyself. Be Thou in the hiddendepths of my heart the one power that keeps me occupied, and holdsme in possession. Let all know of me that Thou art my King, that Iask only for Thy will. In my separation from the world, in mysurrender to Thy people and to Thy will, let it be manifest that Iam wholly, yea, wholly, the Lord's. Amen.

1. There is well-nigh no point of the Christian life in connection with which I should more desire to urge you to pray to God that He may enlighten your eyes, than this of the entire consecration that God desires. In myself and others, I discover that with our own thoughts we can form no conception how completely God Himself would take possession of our will and live in us. The Holy Spirit must reveal this in us. Only then indeed does a conviction arise of how little we understand this. We are not to think: I see truly how entirely I must live for God, but I cannot accomplish this: no, we are to say: I am still blind, I have still no view of what is the glory of a life in which God is all: if I should once see that, I would strongly desire and believe that, not I, but God, should work it in me.

2. Let there not be in your mind the least doubt as to whether you have given yourself to God, to live wholly and only as His. Express this conviction often before Him. Acknowledge that you do not yet see or understand what it means, but abide by this, that you desire it to be so. Reckon on the Holy Spirit to seal you, to stamp you as God's entire possession. Even if you stumble and discover self-will, hold fast your integrity, and trustfully aver that the deep, firm choice of your heart is in all things, in all things, to live to God.

3. Keep always before your eyes that the power to give all to the Lord, and to be all for the Lord, arises from the fact that He has given all for you, that He is all for you. Faith in what He did for you is the power of what you do for Him.

38. Assurance Of Faith

Looking unto the promise of God, Abraham wavered not through unbelief, but waxed strong through faith, giving glory to God, and being fully assured that, what He had promised, He was able also to perform.'—Rom. 4:20,21

My little children, let us not love in word, neither with the tongue; but in deed and truth. Hereby shall we know that we are of the truth, and shall assure our heart before Him.'—1 John 3:18,19

And hereby we know that He abideth in us, by the Spirit which He gave us.'—1 John 3:24

Every child of God has need of the assurance of faith: the full certitude of faith that the Lord has received him and made him His child. The Holy Scripture always speaks to Christians as those that know that they are redeemed, that they are now children of God, and that they have received eternal life. (Deut. 26:27,28; Isa. 44:5; Gal. 4:7; 1 John 5:12) How, pray, can a child love or serve his father, while he is uncertain whether his father will really acknowledge him as a child? We have already spoken on this point in a previous chapter; but oftentimes by ignorance or distrust a Christian again comes into darkness: for this reason we will now deal with it once again of set purpose.

Scripture names three things by which we have our certitude: first, faith in the word; after that, works; and then, in and with both of these, the Holy Spirit.

First, faith in the word. Abraham is to us the great exemplar of faith, and also of the assurance of faith. And what then says the Scripture about the certitude that he had? He was fully assured that what God had promised He was able also to perform. His expectation was only from God, and what God had promised. He relied upon God to do what He had said: the promise of God was for him his only but sufficient assurance of faith. (John 3:33, 5:24; Acts. 27:25; Rom. 4:21,22; 1 John 5:10,11)

There are many young Christians who think that faith in the word is not sufficient to give full certitude: they would fain have something more. They imagine that assurance, a sure inward feeling or conviction, is what is given above or outside of faith This is wrong. As I have need of nothing more than the word of a trustworthy man to give me complete certitude, so must the word of God be my certitude. People err because they seek something in themselves and in their feeling. No: the whole of salvation comes from God: the soul must not be occupied with itself or its work, but with God: he that forgets himself to hear what God says, and to rely upon His promise as something worthy of credit, has in this fact the fullest assurance of faith. (Num. 23:19; Ps. 89:35) He does not doubt the promises, but is strong in faith, giving God the glory, and being fully assured that what was promised God is also able to perform.

Then the Scripture names also works: by unfeigned love we shall assure our hearts. (1 John 3:18,19) Here carefully observe this: assurance by faith in the promise, without works, comes first. The godless man who receives grace knows this only from the word. But then, later on, assurance is to follow from works. By works was faith made perfect.' (John 15:10,14: Gal. 5:6; Jas. 2:22; 1 John 3:14) The tree is planted in faith; without fruits. But when the time of fruit arrives, and no fruit appears, then I may doubt. The more clearly I at the outset hold the assurance of faith, without works, on the word alone, the more certainly shall works follow.

And both—assurance by faith and by works—come by the Spirit. Not by the word alone, and not by works as something that I myself do, but by the word as the instrument of the Spirit, and by works as the fruit of the Spirit, has a child of God the heavenly certification that he is the Lord's. (John 4:13; Rom. 8:13,14; 1 John 3:24)

O let us believe in Jesus as our life, and abide in Him, and assurance of faith shall never be lacking to us.

O my Father, teach me to find my assurance of faith in a life withThee, in cordial reliance upon Thy promises, and in cordialobedience to Thy commands. Let Thy Holy Spirit also witness with myspirit that I am a child of God. Amen.

1. The importance of the assurance of faith lies in the fact, that I cannot possibly love or serve as a child a God of whom I do not know whether He loves and acknowledges me as His child.

2. The whole Bible is one great proof for the assurance of faith. Just because it thus speaks of itself, it is not always named. Abraham and Moses knew well that God had received them: otherwise they could not serve or trust Him. Israel knew that God had redeemed them: for this reason they had to serve God. How much more must this be the case in the greater redemption of the New Testament? All the Epistles are written to men of whom it is presupposed that they know and confess that they are redeemed, holy children of God.

3. Faith and obedience are inseparable, as root and fruit. First, there must be the root, and the root must have time without fruits; then later on come surely the fruits: first assurance without fruits by living faith in the word; then, further assurance from fruits. It is in a life with Jesus that assurance of faith is exalted firmly above all doubt.

4. Assurance of faith is much helped by confession. What I express becomes from me more evident; I am bound and confirmed by it.

5. It is at the feet of Jesus, looking up into His friendly countenance, listening to His loving promises, it is in intercourse with Jesus Himself in prayer, that all doubtfulness of mind falls away. Go thither for the full assurance of faith.

39. Conformity To Jesus

Foreordained to be conformed to the image of His Son.'—Rom. 8:29

I have given you an example, that ye also should do as I have done to you.'—John 13:15

The Bible speaks of a twofold conformity, a twofold likeness that we bear. We may be conformed to the world or to Jesus. The one excludes and drives out the other. Conformity to Jesus, where it is sought, will be secretly prevented by conformity to the world more than anything else. And conformity to the world can be overcome by nothing but conformity to Jesus.

Young Christian, the new life of which you have become partaker is the life of God in heaven. In Christ that life is revealed and made visible. What the workings and fruits of eternal life were in Jesus, they shall also be in you: in His life you get to see what eternal life will work in you. It cannot be otherwise: if for this end you surrender yourself unreservedly to Jesus and the dominion of eternal life, it will bring forth in you a walk of wonderful conformity to that of Jesus. (Matt. 20:27,28; Luke 6:40; John 6:57; 1 John 2:6; 4:17)

To the true imitation of Jesus in His example and growth in inward conformity to Him, two things especially are necessary. These are a clear insight that I am really called to this, and a firm trust that it is possible for me.

One of the greatest hindrances in the spiritual life is that we do not know, that we do not see, what God desires that we should be. (Matt. 22:19; Luke 24:16; 1 Cor. 3:1,2; Heb. 5:11,12) Our understanding is still so little enlightened, we have still so many of our own human thoughts and imaginations about the true service of God, we know so little of waiting for the Spirit who alone can teach us. We do not acknowledge that even the clearest words of God do not have for us the meaning and power that God desires. And so long as we do not spiritually discern what likeness to Jesus is, and how utterly we are called to live like Him, there can be but little said of true conformity. Would that we could only conceive our need of a special heavenly instruction on this point. (1 Cor. 2:12,13; Eph. 1:17,18)

Let us for this end earnestly examine the Scriptures in order to know what God says and desires about our conformity to Christ. (John 13:15; 15:10,12; 27:18; Eph. 5:2; Phil. 2:5; Col. 3:18) Let us unceasingly ponder such words of Scripture, and keep our heart in contact with them. Let it remain fixed with us that we have given ourselves wholly to the Lord, to be all that He desires. And let us trustfully pray that the Holy Spirit would inwardly enlighten us and bring us to a full view of the life of Jesus so far as that can be seen in a believer. (1 Cor. 11:1; 2 Cor. 3:18) The Spirit will convince us that we, no less than Jesus, are absolutely called to live only for the will and glory of the Father: to be in the world even as He is.

The other thing that we have need of is the belief that it is really possible for us with some measure of exactness to bear the image of our Lord. Unbelief is the cause of impotence. We put this matter otherwise. Because we are powerless, we think we dare not believe that we can be conformed to our Lord. This thought is in conflict with the word of God. We do not have it in our own power to carry ourselves after the image of Jesus. No: He is our head and our life. He dwells in us, and will have His life work from within, outwards, with divine power, through the Holy Spirit. (John 14:23; 2 Cor. 13:3; Eph. 3:17,18)

Yet this cannot be apart from our faith. Faith is the consent of the heart, the surrender to Him to work, the reception of His working. Be it unto you according to your faith,' is one of the fundamental laws of the kingdom of God. (Zech. 8:6; Matt 8:29; Luke 1:37,45; 28:27; Gal. 2:20) It is something incredible what a power unbelief has to hinder the working and the blessing of the Almighty God. The Christian who would be partaker of conformity to Christ must specially cherish the firm trust that this blessing is within his reach, is entirely within the range of possibility. He must learn to look to Jesus as Him to whom he by the grace of God Almighty can, in his measure, be really conformable. He must believe that the same Spirit that was in Jesus is also in him; that the same Father that led and strengthened Jesus also watches over him; that the same Jesus that lived on earth now lives in him. He must cherish the strong assurance that this Three-One God is at work in changing him into the image of the Son. (John 14:19; 17:19; Rom. 8:2; 2 Cor. 3:18; Eph. 1:19,10)

He that believes this shall receive it. It will not be without much prayer: it will require especially converse, ceaseless intercourse with God and Jesus. Yet he that desires it and is willing to give time and sacrifice to it, certainly receives it.

Son of God, Effulgence of the glory of God, the very image of Hissubstance, I must be changed into Thine image. In Thee I see theimage and the likeness of God in which we are created, in which weare by Thee created anew. Lord Jesus, let conformity to Thee be theone desire, the one hope of my soul. Amen.

1. Conformity to Jesus: we think that we understand the word: but how little do we comprehend that God really expects we should live even as Jesus. It requires much time with Him, in prayer and pondering of His example, at all rightly to conceive it. The writer of these precepts has written a book on this theme, has often

spoken of it, and yet he sometimes feels as if he must cry out: Is it really true? Has God indeed called us to live even as Jesus?

2. Like Jesus: Thoughts on the image of the Son of God and our conformity to Him,' is the title of a book in which the various features of the image of Jesus and the sure way of receiving them are set forth.

3. Conformity to the world is strengthened especially by intercourse with it: It is in intercourse with Jesus that we shall adopt His mode of thinking, His disposition, His manners.

4. The chief feature of the life of Jesus is this: He surrendered Himself wholly to the Father in behalf of men. This is the chief feature of conformity to Him: the offering up of ourselves to God for the redemption and blessing of the lost.

5. The chief feature His inner disposition was—childlikeness: absolute dependence on the Father, great willingness to be taught, cheerful preparedness to do the will of the Father. Be specially like Him in this.

40. Conformity To The World

I beseech you, brethren, to present your bodies a living sacrifice, holy, acceptable to God. And be not fashioned according to this world: but be ye transformed by the renewing of your mind, that ye may prove what is the good and acceptable and perfect will of God.'—Rom. 12:1,2

Be not conformed to this world. But what is conformity to the world? The opposite of conformity to Jesus: for Jesus and the world stand directly opposed to each other. The world crucified Him. He and His disciples are not of the world. The spirit of this world cannot receive the Spirit of God, for it sees Him not and knows Him not. (John 14:17; 17:14,16; 1 Cor. 2:6,8)

And what is the spirit of this world? The spirit of this world is the disposition that animates mankind in their natural condition, where the Spirit of God has not yet renewed them. The spirit of this world comes from the Evil One, who is the prince of this world, and has dominion over all that are not renewed by the Spirit of God. (John 14:30; 16:11; 1 Cor. 2:12)

And in what does the spirit of this world, or conformity to it, manifest itself? The word of God gives the answer: All that is in the world, the lust of the flesh, and the lust of the eyes, and the vainglory of life, is not of the Father, but is of the world.' The craving for pleasure or the desire to enjoy the world; the craving for property, or the desire to possess the world; the craving for glory, or the desire to be honoured in the world: these are the three chief forms of the spirit of the world. (1 John 2:15,16)

And these three are one in root and essence. The spirit of this world is, that man makes himself his own end: he makes himself the central point of the world: all creation, so far as he has power over it, must serve him; he seeks his life in the visible. This is the spirit of the world: to seek one's self and the visible. (John 5:44) And the Spirit of Jesus: to live not for one's self and not for the visible, but for God and the things that are invisible. (2 Cor. 4:18; 5:7,15)

It is a very terrible and serious thought that once can carry on a busy fashionable life, free from manifest sin or unrighteousness, and yet remain in the friendship of the world, and thereby in enmity against God. (Jas. 4:4)

Where the care for the earthly, for what we eat and what we should drink, for what we possess or may still get into possession, for what we can have brought forth in the earth and made to increase, is the chief element in our life, there we are conformed to this world. It is a terrible and a very serious thought that one can maintain to all appearance a Christian life and think that one is trusting in Christ, while yet one is living with the world for self and the visible. (Matt. 6:32,33) For this reason the command comes to all Christians with great emphasis: Be conformed, not to this world, but to Jesus.

And how can I, for this end, come to be not conformed to the world? Read our text over again with consideration: we read there two things. Observe what goes before. It is those that have presented their bodies to God as a sacrifice on the altar that have it said to them: Be not conformed to the world. Offer yourself to God—that is conformity to Jesus; live every day as one that is offered up to God, crucified in Christ to the world: then you shall not be conformed to the world. (Gal. 6:14)

Observe also what follows: Be transformed by the renewing of your mind, that ye may prove what is the perfect will of God.

There must be a continuous growing renewal of our mind. This takes place by the Holy Spirit, when we let ourselves be led by Him. Then we learn to judge spiritually of what is according to the will of God and what is according to the spirit of the world. A Christian who strives after the progressive renewal of his whole mind shall not be conformed to the world: the Spirit of God makes him conformed to Jesus. (2 Cor. 6:14,16; Eph. 5:17; Heb. 5:14)

Christians, pray, do believe that Jesus has obtained for you the power to overcome the world, with its deep hidden seductions to living for ourselves. Believe this: believe in Him as Victor: and you also have the victory. (John 16:33; 1 John 5:4,5)

Precious Lord, we have presented ourselves to Thee as livingsacrifices. We have offered up ourselves to God. We are not of theworld, even as Thou art not of the world. Lord, let our mind beenlightened by the renewing of the Holy Ghost, that we may rightlysee what the spirit of this world is. And let it be seen in us thatwe are not of this world, but are conformed to Jesus. Amen.

1. Worldly pleasures. Is dancing sin? What harm is there in playing billiards? Why may a Christian not go to the play? One has sometimes wished that there were in the Scriptures a distinct law to forbid such things. God has intentionally not given this. If there were such a law, it would make men only externally pious. God would put each one upon trial whether his inner disposition is worldly or heavenly. Pray, learn Rom. 12:1,2 by heart, and ask the Spirit of God to make it living in you. The Christian who offers himself up to God, and becomes transformed by the renewing of the mind to prove the perfect will of God, will speedily learn whether he may dance or play billiards. The Christian who is afraid only of hell, but not of conformity to the world, cannot see what the Spirit of God gives His children to see.

2. It is remarkable that the trinity of the god of this world, in John's Epistle, is seen as well in the temptation in Paradise as in that of the Lord Jesus.

The lust of the flesh:

The woman saw that the tree was good for food.

Command that those stones become bread.

The lust of the eyes:

And that it was a delight to the eyes.

The devil showeth Him all the kingdoms of the world.

And the vainglory of life.

And that the tree was to be desired to make one wise.

Cast Thyself down.

3. Consider what I say to you: It is only conformity to Jesus that will keep out conformity to the world. Let conformity to Jesus be the study, the endeavour of your soul.

41. The Lord's Day

And God blessed the seventh day, and hallowed it: because that in it He rested from all His work which God had created.'—Gen. 2:3

On that day, the first day of the week, Jesus came and stood in the midst, and saith unto them, Peace be unto you.'—John 20:19

I was in the Spirit on the Lord's day.'—Rev. 1:10

Man abides under the law of time. He must have time for what he would do or obtain. In a wonderful way God gives him time for intercourse with Himself. One day in seven God separated for fellowship with Himself.

The great object of God's gift of this day is said to be, that it may serve as a token that God desires to sanctify man. (Ex. 31:13,17; Ezek. 20:12,20) Endeavour, pray, to understand well that word holy:' it is one of the most important words in the Bible. God is the Holy One: that alone is holy to which God communicates His holiness by revealing Himself thereby. We know that the temple was holy, because God dwelt there. God had taken possession of it. He gave Himself to dwell there. So would God also sanctify man, take possession of him, fill him with Himself, with His own life, His disposition, His holiness. For this end, God took possession of the seventh day, appropriating it to Himself: He sanctified it. And He calls man also to sanctify it, and to acknowledge it as the Lord's day, the day of the Lord's presence and special working. He that does this, that sanctifies this day, shall, as God has promised, be sanctified by Him. (Read with attention Ex. 31:12-17, especially verse 13.)

God blessed the seventh day by sanctifying it. The blessing of God is the power of life, lodged by Him in anything, whereby it has a result full of blessing. Grass, and cattle, and man He blessed with power to multiply. (Gen. 1:22,28; 22:17) And so He lodged in the seventh day a power to bless: the promise that every one that sanctifies this day shall be sanctified and blessed by it. We must accustom ourselves always to think of the Sabbath as a blessed day, that certainly brings blessing. The blessing bound up with it is very great. (Isa. 46:4,7; 48:13,14)

There is still a third word that is used of the institution of the Sabbath: God rested on the seventh day,' and, as it stands in Exodus, was refreshed' or gladdened. God would sanctify and bless us, by introducing us into His rest. He would bring us to see that we are not to burden ourselves with our cares and weakness: we are to rest in Him, in His finished work, in His rest, which He takes because all is in order. This rest is not the outward cessation of employments; no: it is the rest of faith, by which we cease from our works as God did from His, because all is finished. Into this rest we enter by faith in the finished work of Jesus, in surrender to be sanctified by God. (Heb. 4:3,10)

Because Jesus finished the second creation in His resurrection, and we, by the power of His resurrection, enter into life and rest, the seventh day is changed to the first day of the week. There is no specific statement on this point: under the New Testament, the Spirit takes the place of the law. The Spirit of the Lord led His disciples to the celebration of this day. It was the day, not only on which the Lord was raised, but also on which, in all likelihood, the Spirit was poured out: not only on which the Lord manifested Himself during the forty days, but on which the Spirit also specially worked (John 20:1,19,26; Acts. 1:8; 20:7: 1 Cor. 26:2; Rev. 1:10)

The chief lessons that we have to learn about this day are the following:—

The principal aim of the Sabbath is to make you holy, as God is holy. God would have you holy: this is glory, this is blessedness: this is His blessing, this His rest. God would have you holy, filled with Himself and His holiness. (Ex. 29:43,45; Ezek. 37:27,28; 1 Pet. 1:15,16)

In order to sanctify you, God must have you with Him, in His presence and fellowship. You are to come away from all your struggling and working to rest with Him: to rest quietly, without exertion or anxiety, in the certitude that the Son has finished everything, that the Father cares for you in everything, that the Spirit will work everything in you. In the holy rest of a soul that is converted to God, that is silent towards God, that remains silent before His presence to hear what God speaks in him, that reckons upon God to achieve all, God can reveal Himself. (Ps. 52:2,6; Hab. 2:20; Zech. 2:13; John 19:30) It is thus that He sanctifies us.

We sanctify the day of rest, first by withdrawal from all external business and distraction; but then especially by employing it as God's day, belonging to the Lord, for what He destined it, fellowship with Himself.

Take heed, on the other hand, that you do not use the day of rest only as a day for the public observance of divine worship. It is especially in private personal intercourse that God can bless and sanctify you. In the church, the understanding is kept active, and you have the ordinances of preaching, united prayer and praise, to keep you occupied. But we do not there always know whether the heart is really dealing with God, is taking delight in Him. This takes place in solitude. O, accustom yourself, then, to be alone with the Lord your God. Not only speak to Him: let Him speak to you: let your heart be the temple in whose holy silence His voice is heard. Rest in God: then will God say of your heart: This is my rest, here will I dwell. (Ps. 122:13,14)

Young Christian, set great store by the holy, the blessed day of rest. Long for it. Thank God for it. Keep it very holy. And, above all, let it be a day of inner fellowship with your God, of a living converse with His love.

Holy God, I thank Thee for the holy day which Thou givest me as atoken that Thou wilt sanctify me. Lord God, it is Thou who didstsanctify the day by taking it for Thyself: sanctify me in likemanner by taking me for Thyself. Teach me so to enter into Thyrest, so to find my rest in Thy love, that my whole soul shall besilent before Thee, in order that Thou mayest make Thyself and Thylove known in me. And let every Sabbath be to me a foretaste of theeternal rest with Thee. Amen.

1. The Sabbath was the first of all the means of grace, instituted even before the Fall. You cannot see too high a value upon it.

2. Observe how specially the Three-One God has revealed Himself upon the day of rest. The Father rested on this day. The Son rose from the dead upon it. The Spirit sanctified this day by His special workings. You may on this day expect the fellowship and the powerful workings of the Three-One.

3. What is meant by the word holy'? Of what is the day of rest a token, according to Ex. 31:13? How did God sanctify the day of rest? How does He sanctify us?

4. There are in this country peculiar difficulties in the way of the quiet celebration of the day of rest in a village, where the church is often very full. Yet one can lay aside that which is unnecessary and receive the influx of company. We can fix an hour in which there shall be reading and singing.

5. It is a matter of great importance to bring up children aright, for the sanctification of the Sabbath day, by avoiding worldly society and conversation, by accustoming them to read something that may be useful for them. For the younger children, there should be in every place a Sabbath school. For the older children, it would be well to come together in connection with such a book as this,

every one with a Bible, and to review texts.

6. There is no better day than the Lord's day for doing good to body and soul. Let the works of Satan on this day come to an end, and work for the heathen and the ignorant be carried forward.

7. The principal point is this: the day of rest is the day of God's rest, of rest in and with God, and of intercourse with Him. It is God that will sanctify us. He does this by taking possession of us.

42. Holy Baptism

Go ye therefore, and make disciples [5] of all the nations, baptizing them into the name of the Father and of the Son and of the Holy Ghost: teaching them to observe all things whatsoever I commanded you.'—Matt. 28:19

He that believeth and is baptized shall be saved.'—Mark. 26:16

In these words of the institution of baptism, we find its meaning comprehended as in a summary. The word teach' means: make disciples of all the nations, baptizing them.' The believing disciple, as he is baptized in the water, is also to be baptized or introduced into the name of the Three-One God. By the name of the Father, the new birth and life as a child in the love of the Father are secured to him: (Gal. 3:26,27; 4:6,7) by the name of the Son, participation in the forgiveness of sins and the life that is in Christ: (Col. 2:12) by the name of the Holy Spirit, the indwelling and progressive renewal of the Spirit. (Tit. 2:5,6) And every baptized believer must always look upon baptism as his entrance into a covenant with the Three-One God, and as a pledge that the Father, the Son, and the Spirit will in course of time do for him all that they have promised. It requires a life-long study to know and enjoy all the blessing that is presented in baptism.

In other passages of Scripture the thrice two-fold blessing is again set forth separately: thus we find bound up with it the new birth required to make a child of God. Except a man be born of

water and the Sprit, he cannot enter into the kingdom of God.'
The baptized disciple has in God a Father, and he has to live as a
child in the love of this Father. (John 3:3,5)

Then, again, baptism is brought more directly into connection
with the redemption that is in Christ. Consequently, the first and
simplest representation of it is the forgiveness or washing away of
sins. Forgiveness is always the gateway or entrance into all blessing:
hence baptism is also the sacrament of the beginning of the
Christian life; but of a beginning that is maintained through the
whole life. It is on this account that in Rom. 6 baptism is
represented as the secret of the whole of sanctification, the entrance
into a life in union with Jesus. Or are ye ignorant that all we who
were baptized into Christ Jesus were baptized into His death?' And
then follows in verse 4-11, the more precise explanation of what it
is to be baptized into the death of Jesus, and to arise out of this with
Him for a new life in Him. This is elsewhere very powerfully
comprehended in this one word: As many of you as were baptized
into Christ did put on Christ.' This alone is the right life of a
baptized disciple: he has put on Christ. (Rom. 6:3,4; Gal. 3:27;
Col. 2:12) As one is plunged into water and passes under it, so is
the believing confessor baptized into the death of Christ, in order
then to live and walk clothed with the new life of Christ.

And there are other passages where again there is connected
with baptism the promise of the Spirit, not only as the Spirit of
regeneration, but as the gift bestowed from heaven upon believers
for indwelling and sealing, for progressive renewal. He saved us
through the washing of regeneration and renewing of the Holy
Ghost, which He poured out upon us richly.' Renewal is here the
activity of the Spirit, whereby the new life that is planted in the new
birth penetrates our whole being, so that all our thinking and doing
is sanctified by Him. (Rom. 12:2; Eph. 4:23; Tit. 2:5,6)

And all this rich blessing which lies in baptism is received by
faith. He that believeth, and is baptized, shall be saved.' Baptism

was not only a confession on man's part of the faith that he who would be a disciple already had, but equally on God's part a seal for the confirmation of faith, a covenant token in which the whole treasury of grace lay open, to be enjoyed throughout life. As often as a baptized believer sees a baptism administered, or reflects upon it, it is to be to him an encouragement to press by an over-growing faith into the full life of salvation that the Three-One desires to work in him. The Holy Spirit is given to appropriate within us all the love of the Father and all the grace of the Son. The believing candidate for baptism is baptized into the death of Christ, has put on Christ: the Holy Spirit is in him to give him all this as his daily experience. (Eph. 4:14,15; Col 2:16)

Lord God, make Thy holy baptism always operative in my soul as theexperience that I am baptized into the death of Christ. And let Thypeople everywhere understand by Thy Spirit what rich blessing liesthrown open in the baptism of their children. Amen.

And what are we now to think of Infant Baptism? With the assurance that those who cleave only to God's word, namely, the Baptists, will say to us: You cannot adduce a single passage in Scripture where the baptism of little children is spoken of.

Our answer is that this is thoroughly taught us in Scripture, not indeed by separate texts, but by its whole tenor. The reason why the Lord Jesus did not name children specially, was that this was altogether unnecessary. From the time of Abraham onwards God had engrained it in His people, that in His covenant He always reckoned parents and children together. He deals, not with separate individuals alone, but with households: the faith of a father held good for the child, so long as the child did not violate the covenant.

a. In Abraham, Isaac obtained part; in every father amongst the people of Israel his child obtained part in the covenant between Me and thee, and thy seed after thee, to be a God unto thee, and thy seed after thee.' (Gen. 17:7.)b. Even so in connection with the

Passover, it was ordained that, when a stranger would join the people, all his males should be circumcised. (Ex. 12:48)_ Up to the time of Christ it was unquestionably the case that, when any one belonged to the people of God or desired to become attached to them, his little children were received along with him. If the Lord had desired to change this, a very express injunction was needed for the purpose.

c. How expressly did the Lord Jesus declare of children: Of such is the kingdom of God.' And under the kingdom should he not have as a Christian the privilege that he had as a Jew? Yes: the covenant of Abraham is still confirmed from child to child.

d. The answer of Paul to the goal-keeper confirms the continuance of what God had instituted: Believe in the Lord Jesus and thou shalt be saved, and thy house.' Although there were no children in that house, this promise confirms the principle that God deals, not merely with individuals, but with households.

e. Therefore are your children holy.' Since the child itself is holy, it has of itself a right to the holy token of the covenant.

[5] The Dutch version, like our Authorized, has teach' here.

43. The Lord's Supper

The cup of blessing which we bless, is it not a communion of the blood of Christ? The bread which we break, is it not a communion of the body of Christ?'—1 Cor. 10:16

He that eateth My flesh and drinketh My blood abideth in Me, and I in him. He that eateth Me, he also shall live because of Me.'—John 6:56,57

All life has need of food: it is sustained by nourishment which it takes in from without. The heavenly life must have heavenly food; nothing less than Jesus Himself is the bread of life: He that eateth Me shall live by Me.' (Ps. 42:3; Matt. 4:4; John 6:51)

This heavenly food, Jesus, is brought near to us in two of the means of grace, the word and the Lord's Supper. The word comes to present Jesus to us from the side of the intellectual life, by our thoughts. The Lord's Supper comes in like manner to present Jesus to us from the side of the emotional life, by the physical senses. Man has a double nature: he has spirit and body. Redemption begins with the spirit, but it would also penetrate to the body, (Rom. 8:23; 1 Cor. 6:13, 15,19,20; Phil. 3:21) Redemption is not complete until this mortal body also shall share in glory. The Supper is the pledge that the Lord will also change our body of humiliation and make it like His own glorified body by the working whereby He subdues all things to Himself. It is not simply because all that is corporeal is more clear and intelligible for us, that the

Lord gives Himself in the bread of the Supper. No: by the body, Scripture often understands the whole man. In the Supper, Christ would take possession of the whole man, body and soul, to renew and sanctify it by the power of His holy body and blood. Even His body shares in His glory: even His body is communicated by the Holy Spirit. Even our body is fed with His holy body, and renewed by the working of the Holy Spirit. (Matt. 26:26; John 6:54,55; Rom. 8:11,13)

This feeding with the body of Christ takes place, on the side of the Lord by the Spirit, on our side by faith. On the side of the Lord by the Spirit: for the Spirit communicates to us the power of the glorified body, whereby even our bodies, according to Scripture, become members of His body. (1 Cor. 6:15,17; 12:13; Eph. 5:23,30) The Spirit gives us to drink of the life-power of His blood, so that that blood becomes the life and the joy of our soul. The bread is a participation in the body: the cup is a participation in the blood.

And this takes place on our side by faith: a faith that, above what can be seen or understood, reckons on the wonder-working power of the Holy Spirit to unite us really, alike in soul and body, with our Lord, by communicating Him inwardly to us. (Luke 1:37; 1 Cor. 2:9,12)

This is what the Heidelberg Catechism intends in Question and Answer 76.

What is it to eat the glorified body of Christ and to drink His shed blood?'

It is not only to receive with a believing heart the whole suffering and dying of Christ, and thereby to obtain forgiveness of sins and eternal life, but also therewith, by the Holy Spirit, who dwells alike in Christ and in us, to be so united more and more with His blessed body, that we, although He is in heaven and we are upon earth, are nevertheless flesh of His flesh and bone of His bone, and so live and are governed eternally by one Spirit, as the members of our body by a soul.' [6]

This deeply inward union with Jesus, even with His body and blood, is the great aim of the Lord's Supper. All that it teaches and gives us of the forgiveness of sins, of the remembrance of Jesus, of the confirmation of the divine covenant, of union with one another, of the announcement of the Lord's death till He comes, must lead to this: complete oneness with Jesus through the Spirit. (Matt. 26:28; Luke 22:19; John 6:56; 25:4; 1 Cor. 10:17; 11:25; Rev. 3:20) He that eateth My flesh and drinketh My blood abideth in Me, and I in him. He that eateth Me, he shall live by Me.'

It is readily understood that the blessing of the Supper depends very much on preparation within the inner chamber, on the hunger and thirst with which one longs for the living God. (Job. 11:13; Isa. 45:1,3; Matt. 5:6; Luke 1:53; 1 Cor. 11:8) Do not imagine, however, that the Supper is nothing but an emblematic token of what we already have by faith in the word. No: it is a spiritual actual communication from the exalted Lord in heaven of the powers of His life: yet this, only according to the measure of desire and faith. Prepare for the Lord's Supper, therefore, with very earnest separation and prayer. And then expect that the Lord will, with His heavenly power, in a way to you incomprehensible, yet sure, renew your life.

Blessed Lord, who didst institute the Supper in order to communicateThyself to Thy redeemed as their food and their power of life, Oteach us to use the Supper. Teach us at every opportunity to eatand to drink with great hunger and thirst for Thyself and for fullunion with Thee, believing that the Holy Spirit feeds us with Thybody and gives us to drink of Thy blood. Amen.

1. In connection with the Supper let us be especially on our guard against the idea of a mere divine service of the congregation or transitory emotion. Preaching and addresses may make an edifying impression, while there is little power or blessing.

2. For a meal, the first requisite is hunger. A strong hunger and thirst for God is indispensable.

3. In the Supper, Jesus desires to give Himself to us, and would have us give ourselves to Him. These are great and holy things.

4. The lessons of the Supper are many. It is a feast of remembrance; a feast of reconciliation; a covenant feast; a love feast; a feast of hope. But all these separate thoughts are only subordinate parts of the principal element: the living Jesus would give Himself to us in the most inward union. The Son of God would descend into our inmost parts; He would come in to celebrate the Supper with us. He that eateth My flesh and drinketh My blood, let him abide in Me, and I in him.'

5. And then union with Jesus is union with His people in love and sympathy.

6. The preparatory address is not itself the preparation: it is only a help to the private preparation which one must have in intercourse with Jesus.

7. To hold festival with God at His table is something of unspeakable importance. Pray, do not suppose that, because you are a Christian, it is easy for you to go and sit down. No: betake yourself to solitude with Jesus, that He may speak to you and say how you are to prepare you heart to eat with Him, yea, with Himself.

It is very useful to take the whole week before the Supper for preparation and the whole week after for reflection.

[6] Der Heidelbergische Catechismus,' 28, 5:76.

44. Obedience

Now therefore, if ye will obey My voice indeed, ye shall be a peculiar treasure unto Me from among all peoples.'—Ex. 19:5

The Lord will surely bless thee, if thou only diligently hearken unto the voice of the Lord thy God.'—Deut. 25:4,5

By faith Abraham obeyed.—Heb. 11:8

He learned obedience by the things which He suffered; and having been made perfect, He became unto all them that obey Him the author of eternal salvation.'—Heb. 5:8,9

Obedience is one of the most important words in the Bible and in the life of the Christian. It was in the way of disobedience that man lost the favour and the life of God: it is only in the way of obedience that that favour and that life can again be enjoyed. (Rom. 5:19; 6:16; 1 Pet. 1:2,14,22) God cannot possibly take pleasure in those who are not obedient, or bestow His blessing upon them. If ye will obey My voice indeed, ye shall be a peculiar treasure unto Me;' The Lord will surely bless thee, if thou only diligently hearken unto the voice of the Lord thy God.' These are the eternal principles according to which alone man can enjoy God's favour and blessing.

We see this in the Lord Jesus. He says: If ye keep My commandments, ye shall abide in My love; even as I have kept my Father's commandments, and abide in His love.' He was in the love of the Father, but could not abide there otherwise than by

178Andrew Murray

obedience. And He says that this is equally for us the one way to
abide in His love: we must keep His commandments. He came to
open for us the way back to God: this way was the way of
obedience: only he that through faith in Jesus walks in this way
shall come to God. (Gen. 22:17,18; 26:4,5; 1 Sam. 25:22; John
25:10)

How gloriously is this connection betwixt the obedience of Jesus
and our own expressed in Heb. 5: He learned obedience, and
became unto all them that obey Him the author of eternal
salvation.' This is the bond of unity between Jesus and His people,
the point of conformity and inward unanimity. He was obedient to
the Father: they, on the other hand, are obedient to Him. He and
they are both obedient. His obedience not only atones for, but
drives out their disobedience. He and they bear one token:
obedience to God. (Rom. 6:17; 2 Cor. 10:5; Phil. 2:8)

This obedience is a characteristic of the life of faith. It is called
the obedience of faith. (Acts. 6:7; Rom. 1:5; 16:26) There is
nothing in earthly things that so spurs on men to work as faith: the
belief that there is advantage or joy to be found is the secret of all
work. By faith Abraham, when he was called, obeyed:' according to
what I believe shall my works be. The faith that Jesus made me free
from the power of sin for obedience and sets me in a suitable
condition for it, has a mighty power to make me obedient. Faith in
the overflowing blessing which the Father gives to it, faith in the
promises of the love and indwelling of God, of the fulness of the
Spirit which comes by this channel, strengthens for obedience.
(Deut. 28:1; Isa. 63:5; John 14:15,11,23; Acts. 5:32)

The power of this faith, again, as also of obedience lies especially
in intercourse with the living God Himself. There is but one
Hebrew word for obeying voice' and hearing voice:' to hear aright
prepares to obey. It is when I learn the will of God, not in the
words of a man or a book, but from God Himself, when I hear the
voice of God, that I shall surely believe what is promised and do

what is commanded. The Holy Spirit is the voice of God: when we hear the living voice speak, obedience becomes easy. (Gen. 12:1,4; 31:13,16; Matt. 14:28; Luke 5:5; John 10:4,27) O let us then wait in silence upon God, and set our soul open before Him, that He may speak by His Spirit. When in our Bible-reading and praying we learn to wait more upon God, so that we can say: My God has spoken this to me, has given me this promise, has commanded this, then shall we also obey. To listen to the voice' earnestly, diligently, is the sure way to obedience.

With a servant, a warrior, a child, a subject, obedience is indispensable, the first token of integrity. And shall God, the living, glorious God, find no obedience with us? (Mal. 1:6; Matt. 7:21) No: let cheerful, punctual, precise obedience from the beginning be the token of the genuineness of our fellowship with the Son whose obedience is our life.

O Father, who makest us Thy children in Christ, Thou makest us inHim obedient children, as He was obedient. Let the Holy Spirit makethe obedience of Jesus so glorious and powerful in us, thatobedience shall be the highest joy of our life. Teach us ineverything only to seek to know what Thou desirest and then to doit. Amen.

For a life of obedience these things are required:—

1. Decisive surrender. I must no longer have to ask in every single case: Shall I or shall I not, must I, can I, be obedient? No: it must be such an unquestionable thing, that I shall know of nothing else than to be obedient. He that cherishes such a disposition and thinks of obedience as a thing that stands firm, shall find it easy, yea, shall literally taste in it great joy.

2. The knowledge of God's will through the Spirit. Pray, do not imagine that, because you know the Bible in some sort, you know the will of God. The knowledge of God's will is something spiritual: let the Holy Spirit make known to you the knowledge of God's will.

3. The doing of all that we know to be right. All doing teaches men: all doing of what is right teaches men obedience. All that the word, or conscience, or the Spirit tells you is right, actually do it. It helps to form doing into a holy habit, and is an exercise leading to more power and more knowledge. Do what is right, Christian, out of obedience to God, and you shall be blessed.

4. Faith in the power of Christ. You have the power to obey: be sure of this. Although you do not feel it, you have it in Christ your Lord by faith.

5. The glad assurance of the blessing of obedience. It unites us with our God, it wins His good pleasure and love, it strengthens our life, it brings the blessedness of heaven into our heart.

45. The Will Of God

Thy will be done, as in heaven so on earth.'—Matt. 6:10

The glory of heaven, where the Father dwells, is that His will is done there. He who would taste the blessedness of heaven must know the Father who is there, and do His will, as it is done in heaven. (Dan. 4:35)

Heaven is an unending holy kingdom, of which the throne of God is the central point. Around this throne there are innumerable multitudes of pure, free beings, all ordered under powers and dominions. An indescribably rich and many-sided activity fills their life. All the highest and noblest that keeps man occupied is but a faint shadow of what finds place in this invisible world. All these beings possess each their free personal will. The will, however, has in self-conscious freedom, by its own choice, become one with the holy will of the holy Father, so that, in the midst of a diversity that flashes out in a million forms, only one will is accomplished—the will of God. All the rich, blessed movement of the inhabitants of heaven has its origin and its aim in the will of God.'

And why is it then that His children on earth do not regard this will as their highest joy? Wherefore is it that the petition, Thy will be done as in heaven,' is for the most part coupled with thoughts of the severe, the trying elements in the will of God, of the impossibility of our always rejoicing in God's will? The cause is this: we do not take pains to know the will of God in its glory and beauty, as the emanation of love, as the source of power and joy, as the expression of the perfection of God. We think of God's will only in the law that He gave and that we cannot keep, or in the trials in which this will appears in conflict with our own. O let us no longer do this, but take pains to understand that in the will of God all His love and blessedness are comprehended and can be apprehended by us. (Gal. 1:4; Eph. 1:5,9,11; Heb. 10:10)

Hear what the word says about the will of God: and the glorious things that are destined for us in this will.

This is the will of my Father, that every one that beholdeth the Son and believeth on Him should have eternal life.' The will of God is the rescue of sinners by faith in Christ. He that surrenders himself to this glorious will to seek souls shall have the assurance that God will bless his work to others; for he carries out God's will, even as Jesus did it. (John 4:35; 5:30; 6:38,40)

It is not the will of your Father which is in heaven that one of these little ones should perish.' The will of God is the maintenance, the strengthening, the keeping of the weakest of His children. What courage shall he have who unites himself cordially with this will. (Matt. 28:14)

This is the will of God, even your sanctification.' With His whole heart, with all the power of His will, is God willing to make us holy. If we but open our heart to believe that it is not the law, but the will of God, something that He certainly gives and does where we permit Him, then shall we rejoice over our sanctification a stable and sure. (1 Thess. 4:3; 5;23)

In everything give thanks: for this is the will of God in Christ Jesus to you-ward.' A joyful, thankful life is what God has destined for us, is what He will work in us: what He desires, that He certainly does in those who do not withstand Him, but receive and suffer His will to work in them. (1 Thess. 5:18)

What we require then is to surrender our spirit to be filled with the thought, that what God would have He will certainly bring to pass when we do not resist Him. And if we further consider how glorious, and good, and perfect the will of God is, shall we not then yield ourselves with the whole heart, that this will may bring itself to accomplishment in us? (Rom. 12:2)

To this end, let us believe that the will of God is His love. Let us see what blessings in the word are connected with the doing of this will. (Matt. 7:21; 12:50 John 7:17; 9:31; Eph. 5:17; 6:6; 1 John 2:17) Let us think of the glory of heaven as consisting in the doing of God's will, and make the choice that that our life on earth shall be. And let us with prayer and meditation suffer ourselves to be led of the Spirit to know this will aright. (Rom. 12:2; Col. 1:9; 4:12; Heb. 10:36; 13:21)

When we have thus learned to know the will of God on its glorious heavenly side in the word, and have done it, it will not be difficult for us also to bear this will where it appears to be contrary to our nature. We shall be so filled with the adoration of God and His will, that we shall resolve to see, and approve, and love this will in everything. And it will be the most glorious thought of our life that there is to be nothing, nothing, in which the will of God must not be known and honoured. (Ps. 42:9; Matt. 26:39; Heb. 10:7,9)

O my Father, this was the glory of the Lord Jesus, that He did notHis own will, but the will of His Father. This His glory I desireto have as mine. Father, open mine eyes and my heart to know theperfection, the glory of Thy will, and the glory of a life in thiswill. Teach me to understand Thy will aright, then willingly andcheerfully to execute it; and where I have to hear it, to do thisalso with filial adoration. Amen.

1. To do the will of God from the heart in prosperity is the only way to bear this will from the heart in suffering.

2. To do the will of God, I must know it spiritually. The light and the power of the Spirit go together: what He teaches to see as

God's will, He certainly teaches all to do. Meditate much on Rom. 12:2, and pray earnestly to see God's will aright.

3. Learn always to adore the will of God in the least and the worst thing that man does to you. It is not the will of God that His child should be proved thereby. Say then always in the least as well as the greatest trials: It is the will of God that I am in this difficulty. This brings the soul to rest and silence, and teaches it to honour God in the trial. On this point read the chapter, Is God in everything?' In the excellent little book, The Christians Secret of Salvation.' [7]

4. When God gave a will to man, He gave him a power whereby he could accept or reject the will of God. Child of God, pray, open your will to receive the will of God with its full power, and to be filled with it. This is heavenly glory and blessedness, to be conscious every day: my will is in harmony with God's will; God's will lives in me. It is the will of God to work this in you.

[7] [The Christian's Secret of a Happy Life, by H .W. S. F. E. Longely, chap. 8 p. 83.—Translator]

46. Self-Denial

Then said Jesus unto His disciples, If any man would come after Me, let him deny himself, and take up his cross and follow Me.'—Matt. 16:24

Self-denial was an exercise of which the Lord Jesus often spoke. He mentioned it several times as an indispensable token of every true disciple. He connects it with cross-bearing and losing life. (Matt. 10:38,39; Luke 9:23; 14:27; John 12:24,25) Our old life is so sinful, and remains to the end so sinful, that it is never in a condition for anything good. It must therefore be denied and mortified, in order that the new life, the life of God, may have free dominion over us. (Rom. 6:6; 8:13; Gal. 2:20; 5:24; 6:14; Col. 3:5) Let the young Christian resolve from the very beginning to deny himself wholly, in accordance with the injunction of his Lord. At the outset, it seems severe: he will find that it is the source of inconceivable blessing.

Let self-denial reach our carnal understanding. It was when Peter had spoken according to the thought of the natural understanding, that the Lord had to say to him: Thou mindest not the things of God, but the things of men.' You must deny yourselves and your own thoughts. We must be careful that the activity of our understanding with the word and prayer, in endeavouring to reach the knowledge of what is God's will, does not deceive us with a service of God that is not in spirit and in truth. Deny your carnal understanding; bring it to silence; in holy silence give place to the Holy Spirit; let the voice of God be heard in your heart. (Matt. 26:21; 1 Cor. 1:17,27; 2:6; Col. 2:18)

Deny also your own will, with all its lusts and desires. Let it be once for all unquestionable that the will of God in everything is your choice, and that therefore every desire that does not fall in with this will, must be mortified. Pray, believe that in the will of God there is heavenly blessedness, and that therefore self-denial appears severe only at the outset, but, when you exercise yourself heartily in it, becomes a great joy. Let the body with all its life abide under the law of self-denial. (Matt. 26:39; Rom. 6:13; 1 Cor. 9:25,27)

Deny also your own honour. Seek not it, but the honour of God. This brings such a rest into the soul. How can ye believe,' says Jesus, which receive glory one of another?' Although your honour be hurt or reviled, commit it to God to watch over it. Be content to be little, to be nothing. Blessed are the poor in spirit, for theirs is the kingdom.' (John 5:44; 7:18; 8:50; 1 Thess. 2:6)

Deny, in like manner, your own power. Cherish the deep conviction that it is those who are weak, those who are nothing, that God can use. Be very much afraid of your own endeavours in the service of God, however sincere they may be. Although you feel as if you had power, say before God that you have it not, that your power is nothing: continuous denial of your own power is the way to enjoy the power of God. It is in the heart that dies to its own power, that the Holy Spirit decides to dwell and bring the power of God. (2 Cor. 3:5; 12:9)

Deny especially your own interests. Live not to please yourself, but your neighbour. He that seeks his own life shall lose it; he that would live for himself shall not find life. But he that would really imitate Jesus, to share in His joy, let him give his life as He did, let him sacrifice his own interests. (Rom. 15:1,3; 1 Cor. 10:23,24;

Eph. 2:4)

Beloved Christian, at conversion you had to make a choice betwixt your own self and Christ, which you should obey. You then said: Not I, but Christ' Now you are to confirm this choice every day. The more you do so, the more joyful and blessed will it be for you to renounce the sinful self, to cast aside unholy self-working, and suffer Jesus to be all. The way of self-denial is a way of deep heavenly blessedness.

There are very many Christians that observe nothing of this way. They would have Jesus to make them free from punishment, but not to liberate them from themselves, from their own will. But the invitation to discipleship still always rings: If any man would come after Me, let him deny himself, and take up his cross and follow Me.'

The reason as well as the power for self-denial, we find in the little word Me. If any man would come after Me, let him deny himself, and follow Me.' The old life is in ourselves: the new life is in Jesus: the new life cannot rule without driving out the old. Where one's own self had everything to say, it must be nothing. This it would fain not be: on this account there must be all the day denial of one's self, imitation of Jesus. He, with His teaching, His will, His honour, His interests, must fill the heart. But he that has and knows Him, willingly denies himself: Christ is so precious to him, that he sacrifices everything, even himself, to win Him. (Gal. 2:20; Phil. 3:7,8)

This is the true life of faith. Not according to what nature sees or thinks to be acceptable, do I live, but according to what Jesus says and would have. Every day and every hour I confirm the wonderful bargain: Not I, but Christ:' I nothing, Christ everything. Ye died,' and no longer have power, or will, or honour; your life is hid with Christ in God:' Christ's power and will alone prevail. O soul, cheerfully deny that sinful wretched self, in order that the glorious Christ may dwell in you.

Precious Saviour, teach me what self-denial is. Teach me so todistrust my heart that in nothing shall I yield to its fancy. Teachme so to know Thee that it shall be impossible for me to do anythingelse than to offer up myself to possess Thee and Thy life. Amen.

1. Of the denial of the natural understanding Tersteegen says: God and His truth are never known aright, save by such an one as, by the dying of his carnal nature, his inclinations, passions, and will, is made very earnest and silent; and by the abandonment of the manifold deliberations of the understanding, has become very simple and childlike. We must give our heart and our will entirely to God, forsaking our own will in all things, releasing ourselves especially from the manifold imaginations and activities of the understanding, even in spiritual things, that it may collect itself silently in the heart, and dwell as in the heart with God. Not in the head, but in the heart is found the living truth itself, the anointing that teaches us all things. In the heart is found the living fountain of light. Any one that lives in a heart entertained with God, will often with a glance of the eye discern more truth than another with the greatest exertion.'

2. Read the above passage with care: you will find in it the reason why we have several times said, that when you read or pray you must at every opportunity keep quiet for a little and set yourself in entire silence before God. This is necessary, to bring the activity of the natural understanding to silence and to set the heart open before God, that He may speak there. In the heart is the temple where worship in spirit and truth takes place. Distrust, deny your understanding in spiritual things. The natural understanding is in the head: the spiritual understanding is in the heart, the temple of God. O preserve in the temple of God a holy silence before His countenance: then He will speak.

3. The peculiar mark of Christian self-denial is inward cheerfulness and joy in the midst of privation. The word of God

makes unceasing joy a duty. This gladsome disposition, which, hailing from eternity, has all change and vicissitude under foot, will hold its ground, not only in times of severe suffering, but also in the self-denial of every day and hour that is inseparable from the Christian life.'

4. What all am I to deny? Deny yourself. How shall I know where and when to deny myself? Do so always and in everything. And if you do not rightly understand that answer, know that no one can give you the right explanation of it but Jesus Himself. To imitate Him, to be taught of Him, is the only way to self-denial. Only when Jesus comes in, does self go out.

47. Discretion

For wisdom shall enter into thine heart, and knowledge shall be pleasant unto thy soul; discretion shall watch over thee, understanding shall keep thee.'—Prov. 2:10,11

My son, keep sound wisdom and discretion: so shall they be life unto thy soul.'—Prov. 3:21,22

Ye ought to be quiet, and to do nothing rash.'—Acts. 19:36

Indiscretion is not merely the sin of the unconverted: amongst the people of God, it is often the cause of much evil and misery. We read of Moses: They angered him also at the waters of Meribah, so that it went ill with Moses for their sakes: because they were rebellious against his spirit, and he spake unadvisedly with his lips.' So of Uzzah's touching the ark: And God smote him there for his error' (margin, rashness). (2 Sam. 6:7; Ps. 106:38; Prov. 12:18)

What discretion is, and why it is so necessary, may be easily explained. When an army marches into the province of an enemy, its safety depends on the guards which are set, which are to be always on the watch, to know and to give warning when the enemy approaches. Advance guards are sent out that the territory and power of the enemy may be known. This prudence, which looks out beforehand and looks round, is indispensable.

The Christian lives in the province of the enemy. All that surrounds him may become a snare or an occasion of sin. Therefore his whole walk is to be carried out in a holy reserve and watchfulness, in order that he may do nothing indiscreet. He watches and prays that he may not enter into temptation. (Matt. 26:41: Luke 1:36; Eph. 6:18; 1 Pet. 4:7; 5:8) Prudence keeps guard over him. (1 Sam. 18:14; Matt. 10:16; Luke 1:17; 16:8; Eph. 5:15; Tit. 2:4)

Discretion keeps watch over the lips. O what loss many a child of God suffers by the thought that if he only speaks nothing wrong, he may speak what he will. He knows not how, through much speaking, the soul becomes ensnared in the distractions of the world, because in the multitude of words there is not wanting transgression. Discretion endeavours not to speak, save for the glory of God and blessing to neighbours. (Ps. 39:2; 141:3; Prov. 10:19; Eccles. 5:1,2)

Over the ear also discretion keeps guard. Through the gate of the ear comes to me all the news of the world, all the indiscreet speech of others, to infect me. Very hurtful for the soul is eagerness for news. One can afterwards no more look into one's self: one lives wholly in the world round about. Corinth was much more godless than Athens; but in this last place, where they spent their time in nothing else but either to tell or to hear some new thing,' very few were converted. Take heed, says Jesus, what ye hear. (Prov. 2:2; 18:15; Mark 4:24; Acts. 17:21)

On this account, discretion keeps watch over the society in which the Christian mingles. He that separateth himself seeketh his own desire.' The child of God has no the freedom to yield himself to the society of the world so much and so long as he would: he must know the will of his Father. (Ps. 1:1; Prov. 28:1; 2 Cor. 6:14; 2 Thess. 3:14; 2 John 10,11)

Discretion keeps watch over all lawful occupations and possessions.It knows how gradually and stealthily the love of money, worldly-mindedness, the secret power of the flesh, obtains the upper hand, and that it can never reckon itself free from this temptation. (Matt. 13:22; Luke 21:34; 1 Tim. 6:9,17)

And, above all, it keeps watch over the heart, because there are the issues of life, there is the fountain out of which everything springs. Remembering the word, he that trusteth in his own heart is a fool,' it walks in deep humility, and it works out salvation with fear and trembling. (Prov. 3:21,23; 4:23; 28:16; Jer. 31:33)

And whence has the soul the power to be with a never-resting watchfulness on its guard against the thousand dangers that surround it on all sides? Is it not fatiguing, exhausting, harassing, to have thus to watch always and never to be at rest in the certainty that there is no danger? No: absolutely not. Discretion brings just the highest restfulness. It has its security and strength in its heavenly Keeper, who slumbers not nor sleeps. In confidence in Him, under the inspiration of His Spirit, discretion does its work: the Christian walks as one that is wise; the dignity of a holy prudence adorns him in all his actions. The rest of faith, the faith that Jesus watches and guards, binds to Him in love, and holy discretion springs as of its own accord from a love that would not grieve or abandon Him, from a faith that has its strength for everything in Him.

O Lord my God, guard me, that I may not be of the indiscreet inheart. Let the prudence of the righteous always characterize me, inorder that in everything I may be kept from giving offense. Amen.

1. To one who bestowed great care on having his horse and cart in thoroughly good order, it was once said: Come, it is not necessary to be always taking so much pains with this. His answer was: I have always found my prudence paid. How many a Christian has need of this lesson. How many a young Christian may well pray for this—that his conversion may be, according to God's word, to the prudence of the righteous.'

2. Discretion has its root in self-knowledge. The deeper my knowledge of my impotence and the sinfulness of my flesh is, the greater is the need of watchfulness. It is thus our element of true

self-denial.

3. Discretion has its power in faith: the Lord is our Keeper, and He does His keeping through the Spirit keeping us in mind. It is from Him that our discretion comes.

4. Its activity is not limited to ourselves: it reaches out especially to our neighbour, in the way of giving him no offense, and in laying no stumbling-block in his way. (Rom. 14:13; 1 Cor. 8:9; 10:32; Phil. 1:10)

5. It finds great delight in silence, so as to commit its way to the Lord with composure and deliberation. It esteems highly the word of the town-clerk of Ephesus: Ye ought to be quiet, and to do nothing rash.'

6. In great generals and their victories, we see that discretion is not timidity: it is consistent with the highest courage and the most joyful certitude of victory. Discretion watches against rashness, but enhances the courage of faith.

48. Money

Money answereth all things.'—Eccles. 10:19

I verily dedicate the silver unto the Lord from my hand.'—Judg. 17:3

Thou oughtest therefore to have put my money to the bankers, and at my coming I should have received back mine own with interest.'—Matt. 25:27

It is in his dealing with the world and its possessions, that the Christian finds one of the opportunities in which he is to manifest his self-denial and the spirit of discretion. (John 17:15,16; 1 Cor. 7:31) Since it is in money that all value or property on earth will finds its expression, so it is especially in his dealing with money that he can show whether he is free from worldliness to deny himself and to serve his God. In order rightly to comprehend this, we must consider for a little what falls to be said about money.

What is money the token of? It is the token of the work by which a man earns it: of his industry, and zeal, and ability in that work: of his success and the blessing of God upon the work. It is also the token of all that I can do with money: the token of the work that others would do for me, of the power that I thereby have to accomplish what I desire, of the influence which I exercise on those that are dependent upon me for my money: a token of all the possessions or enjoyments that are to be obtained by money: a token of all upon earth that can make life desirable: yea, a token of life itself, which without the purchase of indispensable food cannot be supported.

Money is thus, indeed, of earthly things, one of the most desirable and fruitful. No wonder that it is thus esteemed by all.

What is the danger of money? What is the sin that is done with it, that the Bible and experience should so warn us to be prudent in dealing with it? There is the anxiousness that knows not if there will be sufficient money. (Matt. 6:31) There is the coveteousness that longs too much for it. (1 John 2:16) There is the dishonesty that, without gross deception or theft, does not give to a neighbour what belongs to him. (Jas. 5:4) There is the lovelessness that would draw everything to one's self and does not keep another. (Luke 16:21) There is love of money, which seeks after riches and lands in avarice. (1 Tim. 6:9,10,17) There is robbery of God and the poor in withholding the share that belongs to them. (Prov. 7:24,26; Ma. 3:8)

What is the blessing of money? If the danger of sin is so great, would it not be better if there were no money? Is it not better to be without money? No: even for the spiritual life money may be a great blessing: as an exercise in industry and activity, (Prov. 13:4; 18:19) in care and economy: as a token of God's blessing upon our work: (Prov. 10:4,22) as an opportunity for showing that we can possess and lay it out for God, without withholding it or cleaving to it; that by means of it we can manifest our generosity to the poor and our overflowing love for God's cause: (Isa. 47:7,8,10,11; 2 Cor. 8:14,15) as a means of glorifying God by our beneficence, and of spreading among men the gold of heavenly blessing: (2 Cor. 9:12,13) as a thing that, according to the assurance of Jesus, we can exchange for a treasure in heaven. (Matt. 19:21; Luke 12:33)

And what is now the way to be freed from the danger and to be led into the right blessing of money?

Let God be Lord over your money. Receive all your money with thanksgiving, as coming from God in answer to the prayer: Give us this day our daily bread.' (1 Chron. 29:14)

Lay it all down before God as belonging to Him. Say with the woman: I verily dedicate the silver unto the Lord.' (1 Tim. 4:4,5)

Let your dealing with your money be a part of your spiritual life. Receive, and possess, and give out your money as one who has been bought at a high price, redeemed, not with silver and gold, but with the precious blood. (Luke 19:8)

Make what the word of God says of money, of earthly good, a special study. The word of the Father alone teaches how the child of the Father is to use blessing.

Reflect much on the fact that it is not given to you for yourself alone, but for you and your brethren together. The blessing of money is to do good to others, and make them rejoice.

Remember especially that it can be given up to the Father and the service of His kingdom for the upbuilding of His spiritual temple, for the extension of His sway.Every time of spiritual blessing mentioned in Scripture was a time of cheerful giving for God's cause. Even the outpouring of the Holy Spirit make itself known in the giving of money for the Lord. (Ex. 36:5; 1 Chron. 29:6,9; Acts. 2:15; 4:34)

Christian, understand it: all the deepest deliberations of the heart and its most spiritual activities can manifest themselves in the way in which we deal with our money. Love to God, love to our neighbour, victory over the world by faith, the hope of everlasting treasure, faithfulness as steward, joy in God's service, cheerful self-denial, holy discretion, the glorious freedom of the children of God, can all be seen in the use of money. Money can be the means of the most glorious fellowship with God, and the full enjoyment of the blessedness of being able to honour and serve Him.

Lord God, make me rightly discern in what close connection my moneystands with my spiritual life. Let the Holy Spirit lead andsanctify me, so that all my earning and receiving, my keeping anddispensing of money may always be well-pleasing to Thee and ablessing to my soul. Amen.

1. John Wesley always said that there were three rules about the use of money which he gave to men in business, and by which he was sure that they would experience benefit.

Make as much money as you can. Be industrious and diligent.

Save as much money as you can. Be no spendthrift, live frugally and prudently.

Give away as much money as you can. That is the divine destination of money;that makes it an everlasting blessing for yourselves and others.

2. Acquaint yourself with the magnificent prayer of David in 1 Chron. 29. Receive it into your soul; it teaches us the blessedness and the glorification of God that spring from cheerful giving.

49. The Freedom Of The Christian

Being made free from sin, ye became bond-servants of righteousness. Being made free from sin, ye have your fruit unto sanctification.'—Rom. 6:18,22

But now we have been discharged from the law.'—Rom. 7:6

The law of the Spirit of life in Christ Jesus made me free from the law of sin and of death.'—Rom. 8:2

Freedom is counted in Scripture as one of the greatest privileges of the child of God. There is nothing in history for which nations have made great sacrifices except freedom. Slavery is the lowest condition into which man can sink, for in it he can no longer dispose of himself. Freedom is the deepest need of his nature.

To be free, then, is the condition in which anything can develop itself according to the law of its nature, that is, according to its disposition. Without freedom nothing can attain its destiny or become what it ought to be. This is true alike of the animal and man, of the corporeal and the spiritual. It was for this cause that God in Israel chose the redemption out of the slavery of Egypt into the glorious liberty of God's people, as the everlasting type of redemption out of the slavery of sin into the liberty of the children of God. (Ex. 1:14; 4:23; 6:5; 20:2; Deut. 24:8) On this account, Jesus said on earth: If the Son shall make you free, ye shall be free indeed.' And the Holy Scriptures teach us to stand fast in the freedom with which Christ made us free. A right insight into this freedom opens up to us one of the greatest glories of the life that the grace of God has prepared for us. (John 8:32,36; Gal. 4:21,31; 5:1)

In the three passages, from the Epistle to the Romans, in which sanctification is dealt with, a threefold freedom is spoken of. There is freedom from sin in the sixth chapter, freedom from the law in the seventh, freedom from the law of sin in the eighth.

There is freedom from sin (Rom. 6:7,18,22). Sin is represented as a power that rules over man, under which he is brought and taken captive, and that urges him as a slave to evil. (John 8:34; Rom. 7:14,23; 2 Pet. 2:19) By the death of Christ and in Christ of the believer, who is one with Him, he is made entirely free from the dominion of sin: it has no more power over him. If, then, he still does sin, it is because he, not knowing his freedom by faith, permits sin still to rule over him. But it by faith he fully accepts what the word of God thus confirms, then sin has no power over him: he overcomes it by the faith that he is made free from it. (Rom. 5:21; 6:12,14)

Then there is freedom from the law. This leads us deeper into the life of grace than freedom from sin. According to Scripture, law and sin always go together. The strength of sin is the law:' The law does nothing but make the offense greater. (Rom. 4:15; 5:13,20; 7:13; 1 Cor. 15:56) The law is the token of our sinfulness, cannot help us against sin, but with its demand for perfect obedience gives us over hopeless to the power of sin. The Christian who does not discern that he is made free from the law will still always abide under sin. (Rom. 6:15; 7:5) Christ and the law cannot rule over us together: in every endeavour to fulfil the law as believers, we are taken captive by sin. (Rom. 7:5,23) The Christian must know that he is entirely free from the law, from the you must that stands without us and over us: then for the first time shall he know what it is to be free from sin.

Then there is also freedom from the law of sin, actual liberation from the power of sin in our members. What we have in Christ, freedom from sin and from the law, is inwardly appropriated for us by the Spirit of God. The law of the Spirit of life in Christ Jesus made me free from the law of sin and of death.' The Holy Spirit in us takes the place of the law over us. If ye are led of the Spirit, ye are not under the law.' Freeing from the law is not anything external, but takes place according to the measure the Spirit obtains dominion in us and leads us. Where the Spirit of the Lord is, there is liberty.' According as the law of the Spirit rules in us, we are made free from the law, from the law of sin. We are then free to do what we, as God's children, would fain do, free to serve God. (2 Cor. 3:17; Gal. 5:18)

Free expresses a condition in which nothing hinders me from being what I would be and ought to be. In other words, free is to be able to do what I would. The power of sin over us, the power of the law against us, the power of the law of sin in us, hinder us. But he that stands in the freedom of the Holy Spirit, he that is then truly free, nothing can prevent or hinder him from being what he would be and ought to be. As it is the nature of a tree to grow upwards, and it also grows as it is free from all hindrances, so a child of God then grows to what he ought to be and shall be. And according as the Holy Spirit leads him into this freedom, there springs up the joyful consciousness of his strength for the life of faith. He joyfully shouts: I can do all things in Him that strengtheneth me.' Thanks be unto God which always leadeth us in triumph in Christ.'

Son of God, anointed with the Spirit to announce freedom to thecaptives, make me also truly free. Let the Spirit of life in Thee,my Lord, make me free from the law of sin and of death. I am Thyransomed one. O let me live as Thy freed one, who is hindered bynothing from serving Thee. Amen.

1. The freedom of the Christian extends over his whole life. He is free in relation to the institutions and teachings of men. Ye were bought with a price: become not bond-servants of men.' (1 Cor. 7:23; Col. 2:20) He is free in relation to the world, and in the use

of what God gives: he has power to possess it or to dispense with it, to enjoy it or to sacrifice it. (1 Cor. 8:8; 9:4,5)

2. This freedom is no lawlessness. We are free from sin and the law to serve God in the Spirit. We are not under the law, but give ourselves, with free choice and in love, to Him who loved. us. (Rom. 6:18; Gal. 5:13; 1 Pet. 2:16) Not under the law, also not without law; but in the law; a new, a higher law, The law of the Spirit of life,' the law of liberty,' the law written in our hearts, is our rule and measure. (1 Cor. 9:21; Jas. 1:15; 2:12) In this last passage the translation ought to be: bound by a law to Christ.'

3. This freedom has its subsistence from the word and also in it: the more the word abides in me, and the truth lives in me, the freer I become. (John 8:31,32,36)

4. Freedom manifests itself in love. I am free from the law, and from men, and from institutions, to be able now like Christ to surrender myself for others. (Rom. 14:13,21; Ga. 5:13; 6:1)

5. This glorious liberty to serve God and our neighbour in love is a spiritual thing. We cannot by any means seize it and draw it to us. It becomes known only by a life in the Holy Spirit. Where the Spirit of the Lord is there liberty.' If ye are led by the Spirit, ye are not under the law.' It is the Holy Spirit that makes free. Let us suffer ourselves to be introduced by Him into the effectual glorious liberty of the children of God. The Spirit of life in Christ Jesus freed me from the law of sin and of death.'

50. Growth

So is the kingdom of God, as if a man should cast seed upon the earth; and should sleep and rise night and day, and the seed should spring up and grow, he knoweth not how. The earth beareth fruit of herself; first the blade, then the ear, then the full corn in the ear.'—Mark 4:26-28

The Head, from whom the whole body increaseth with the increase of God'—Col. 2:19

That we may grow into Him which is the Head, even Christ, from whom the whole body maketh the increase.'—Eph. 4:15,16

Death is always a standing still: life is always movement, progressiveness. Increase or growth is the law of all created life; consequently, the new life in man is destined to increase, and always by becoming stronger. As there are in the seed and in the earth a life and power of growth by which the plant is impelled to have its full height and fruit; so is there in the seed of the eternal life an impelling force by which also that life always increases and grows with a divine growth, until we come to a perfect man, to the measure of the stature of the fulness of Christ. (Eph. 4:12; 2 Thess. 1:4)

I this parable of the seed that springs up of itself, and becomes great and bears fruit, the Lord teaches us two of the most important lessons on the increase of the spiritual life. The one is that of its self-sufficiency, the other that of its gradualness.

The first lesson is for those that ask what they are to do in order to grow and advance more in grace. As the Lord said of the body: Which of you by being anxious can add one cubit unto his stature? consider the lilies of the field how they grow;' so He says to us here that we can do nothing, and need to do nothing, to make the spiritual life grow. (Hos. 14:16; Matt. 6:25,27,28) Do you not see how, while man slept, the seed sprang up and became high, he knew not how, and how the earth brought forth fruit of itself? When man has once sowed, he must reckon that God cares for the growth: he has not to care: he must trust and rest.

And must man then do nothing? He can do nothing: it is from within that the power of life must come: from the life, from the Spirit implanted in him. To the growth itself he can contribute nothing: it shall be given him to grow. (Ps. 92:14; Gal. 2:20; Col. 3:3)

All that he can do is to let the life grow. All that can hinder the life, he must take away and keep away. If there are thorns and thistles that take away place and power in the soil which the plant should have, he can take them away. (Jer. 4:13; Matt. 13:22,23) The plant must have its place in the earth alone and undivided. For this the husbandman can care: then it grows further of itself. So must the Christian take away what can hinder the growth of the new life: to surrender the heart entire and undivided for the new life, to hold it alone in possession and to fill it, so that it may grow free and unhindered. (Son. 2:15; Heb. 12;1)

The husbandman can also bring forward what the plant requires in the way of food or drink: he can manure or moisten the soil as it may be needful. So must the believer see to it that for the new life there is brought forward nourishment out of the word, the living water of the Spirit, by prayer. It is in Christ that the new life is planted: from Him it increases with divine increase: abide rooted in Him by the exercise of faith: the life will grow of itself. (2 John 15:4,5; Col. 2:6,7) Give it what it must have: take away what can

Andrew Murray

hinder it: the life will grow and increase of itself.

Then comes in the second lesson of the parable: the gradualness of the growth: first the blade, then the ear, then the full corn in the ear.' Do not expect everything at once. Give God time. By faith and endurance we inherit the promises: the faith that knows that it has everything in Christ: the endurance that expects everything in its time according to the rule and the order of the divine government. Give God time. Give the new life time. It is by continued abiding in the earth that the plant grows: it is by continuous standing in grace, in Christ Himself, in whom God has planted us, that the new life grows. (Heb. 3:13; 6:12,15; Jas. 5:7)

Yes: give the new life only sufficient time: time in prayer: time in intercourse with God: time in continuous exercise of faith: time in persistent separation from the world. Give it time: slow but sure, hidden but real, in apparent weakness but with heavenly power, is the divine growth with which the life of God in the soul grows up to the perfect man in Christ.

Lord God, graciously strengthen the faith of Thy children, that their growth and progress are in Thy hands. Enable them to see what a precious, powerful life was implanted in them by Thyself, a life that increases with a divine increase. Enable them by faith and patience to inherit the promises. And teach them in that faith to take away all that can hinder the new life, to bring forward all that can further it, so that Thou mayest make Thy work in them glorious. Amen.

1. For a plant, the principal thing is the son in which it stands and out of which it draws its strength. For the Christian, this also is the principal thing: he is in Christ. Christ is all: he must grow up in Him, for out of Him the body obtains its increase. To abide in Christ by faith—that is the main thing.

2. Remember that faith must set itself towards a silent restfulness, that growth is just like that of the lilies on God's hands, and that He will see to it that we increase and grow strong.

3. By this firm and joyful faith, we become Strengthened with all power according to the might of His glory, unto all patience and long-suffering with joy.' (Col. 1:11)

4. This faith, that God cares for our growth, takes away all anxiety, and gives courage for doing the two things that we have to do: the taking away of what may be obstructive to the new life, the bringing forward of what may be serviceable to it.

5. Observe well the distinction betwixt planting and growing. Planting is the work of a moment: in a moment the earth receives the seed: after that comes the slow growth. Without delay—immediately must the sinner receive the word: before conversion there is no delay. Then with time follows the growth of the seed.

6. The main thing is Christ: from Him and in Him is our growth. He is the soil that of itself brings forth fruit, we know not how. Hold daily intercourse with Him.

There is a book Abide in Christ' (Nisbet & Co.), with meditations for a month on the blessed life of continued fellowship with Him.

51. Searching The Scriptures

O how love I Thy law: it is my meditation all the day.'—Ps. 119:97

Ye search (or search ye) the Scriptures: and these are they which bear witness of Me.'—John 5:39

The word did not profit them, because they were not united by faith with them that heard.'—Heb. 4:2

At the beginning of this book there is more than one passage upon the use of God's word in the life of grace. Ere I take leave of my readers, I would fain once again come back to this all-important point. I cannot too earnestly and urgently address this call to my beloved young brothers and sisters: Upon your use of the word of God your spiritual life in great measure depends. Man lives by the word that proceedeth from the mouth of God. Therefore seek with your whole heart to learn how to use God's word aright. To this end, receive the following hints.

Read the word more with the heart than with the understanding: with the understanding I would know and comprehend; with the heart I desire, and love, and hold fast. Let the understanding be the servant of the heart. Be much afraid of the understanding of the carnal nature, that cannot receive spiritual things. (1 Cor. 1:12,27; 2:6,12; Col. 2:18) Deny your understanding, and wait in humility on the Spirit of God. On every occasion, still keep silent amidst your reading of the word, and say to yourselves: this word I now receive in my heart, to love and to let it live in me. (Ps. 119:10,11,47; Rom. 10:8; Jas. 1:21)

Read the word always in fellowship with the living God. The power of a word depends on my conviction regarding the man from whom it comes. First set yourself in loving fellowship with the living God under the impression of His nearness and love: deal with the word under the full conviction that He, the eternal God, is speaking with you; and let the heart be silent to listen to God, to God Himself. (Gen. 17:3; 1 Sam. 3:9,10; Isa. 50:4; 52:6; Jer. 1:2) Then the word certainly becomes to you a great blessing.

Read the word, as a living word in which the Spirit of God dwells, and that certainly works in those that believe. The word is seed. Seed has life, and grows and yields fruit of itself. The word has life, and of itself grows and yields fruit. (Mark 4:27,28; John 6:63; 1 Thess. 2:13; 1 Pet. 1:23) If you do not wholly understand it, if you do not feel its power, carry it in your heart; ponder it and meditate upon it: it will of itself begin to yield a working and growth in you. (Ps. 119:15,40,48,69; 2 Tim. 3:16,17) The Spirit of God is with and in the word.

Read it with the resolve to be, not only a hearer, but a doer of the word. Let the great question be: What would God now have of me with this word? If the answer is: He would have me believe it and reckon upon Him to fulfil it: do this immediately from the heart. If the word is a command of what you are to do, yield yourself immediately to do it. (Matt. 5:19,20; 7:21,24; Luke 11:28; Jas. 1:21,25) O there is an unspeakable blessedness in the doing of God's word, and in the surrender of myself to be and to act just as the word says and would have it. Be not hearers, but doers of the word.

Read the word with time. I see more and more that one obtains nothing on earth without time. Give the word time. Give the word time, at every occasion on which you sit down to read it, to come into your heart. Give it time, in the persistence with which you cleave to it, from day to day, and month after month. (Deut. 6:5;

Ps. 1:2; 119:97; Jer. 15:16) By perseverance you become exercised and more accustomed to the word: the word begins to work. Pray, be not dispirited when you do not understand the word. Hold on: take courage: give the word time: later on the word will explain itself. David had to meditate day and night to understand it.

Read the word with a searching of the Scriptures. The best explanation of the Bible is the Bible itself. Take three or four texts upon a point: set them close to one another and compare them. See wherein they agree and wherein they differ; where they say the same thing or again something else. Let the word of God at one time be cleared up and confirmed by what He said at another time on the same subject: this is the safest and the best explanation. Even the sacred writers use this method of instruction with the Scriptures: and again.' (Isa. 34:16; John 19:37; Acts. 17:11; Heb. 2:13) Do not complain that this method takes too much time and pains: it is worthy of the pains: your pains will be rewarded. On earth you have nothing without pains. (Prov. 2:4,5; 3:13,18; Matt. 13:44) Even the bread of life we have to eat in the sweat of our face. He that would go to heaven never goes without taking pains. Search the Scriptures: it will be richly recompensed to you.

Young Christian, let one of my last and most earnest words to you be this: on your dealing with the word of God depend your growth, your power, your life. Love God's word then; esteem it sweeter than honey: better than thousands of gold or silver. In the word, God can and will reveal His heart to you. In the word, Jesus will communicate Himself and all His grace. In the word, the Holy Spirit will come in to you, to renew your heart and all your thoughts, according to the mind and will of God. O, then, read not simply enough of the word to keep you from declension, but reckon it one of your chief occupations on earth to yield yourself that God may fill you with His word, that He may fulfil His word in you.

Lord God, what grace it is that Thou speakest to us in Thy word, that we in Thy word have access to Thy heart, to Thy will, to

Thylove. O forgive us our sins against Thy precious word. And, Lord,let the new life become so strong by the Spirit in us, that all itsdesire shall be to abide in Thy word. Amen.

1. Ps. 119. In the middle of the Bible stands this psalm, in which the praise and the love of God's word are so strikingly expressed. It is not enough for us to read through the divisions of this psalm successively: we must take its principal points, and one with another seek what is said in different passages upon each of these. Let us, for example, take the following points, observing the indications of the answers, and seek in this way to come under the full impression of what is taught us of the glory of God's word:—

1. The blessing that the word gives. Verses,1,2,6,9,11,14,24,45,46,47, and so on.

2. The appellations that in this psalm are given to God's word.

3. How we have to handle the word. (Observe—walk—keep—mark—and so on.)

4. Prayer for divine teaching. Verses 5,10,12,18,19,26.

5. Surrender to obedience to the word. Verses93,105,106,112,128,133.

6. God's word the basis of our prayer. Verses41,49,58,76,107,116,170.

7. Observance as the ground of confidence in prayer. Verses77,159,176.

8. Observance as promised upon the hearing of prayer. Verses8,17,33,32,44.

9. The power to observe the word. Verses 32,36,41,42,117,135,146.

10. The praise of God's word. Verses 54,72,97,129,130,144.

11. The confident confession of obedience. Verses 102,110,121,168.

12. Personal intercourse with God, seen in the use of Thou and I,Thine and Mine.

I have merely mentioned a few points and a few verses. Seek out more and mark them, until your mind is filled with the thoughts about the word, which the Spirit of God desires to give you.

Read with great thoughtfulness the words of that man of faith, George Mueller. He says: The power of our spiritual life will be according to the measure of the room that the word of God takes up in our life and in our thoughts.' After an experience of fifty-four years, I can solemnly declare this. For three years after my conversion I used the word little. Since that time I searched it with diligence, and the blessing was wonderful. From that time, I have read the Bible through a hundred times in order, and at every time with increasing joy. Whenever I start a fresh with it, it appears to me as a new book. I cannot express how great the blessing is of faithful, daily, regular searching of the Bible. The day is lost for me, on which I have used no rounded time for enjoying the word of God.

Friends sometimes say: I have so much to do, that I can find no time for regular Bible study. I believe that there are few that have to work harder than I have. Yet it remains a rule with me never to begin my work until I have had real sweet fellowship with God. After that I give myself heartily to the business of the day, that is, to God's work, with only intervals of some minutes of prayer.'

52. The Lord The Perfecter

I will cry unto God most High; unto God that performeth all things for me.'—Ps. 57:2

The Lord will perfect that which concerneth me.'—Ps. 138:8

Being confident of this very thing, that He which began a good work in you will perfect it until the day of Jesus Christ.'—Phil. 1:6

For of Him, and through Him, and unto Him are all things. To Him be the glory for ever and ever.'—Rom. 11:36

We read that David was once dispirited by unbelief, and said: I shall one day perish by the hand of Saul.' So even the Christian may indeed fear that he shall one day perish. This is because he looks upon himself and what is in him, and does not set his trust wholly upon God. It is because he does not yet know God as the Perfecter. He does not yet know what is meant by His name being: I am the Alpha and the Omega: the Beginning and the End: the First and the Last.' If I really believe in God as the beginning out of whom all is, then must I also trust Him as the continuation by whom, as also the End to whom, all is.

God is the beginning: He who began a good work in you:' Ye have not chosen Me, but I have chosen you.' It is God's free choice, from before the foundation of the world, that we have to thank that we became believers, and have the new life. (John 15:16; Rom. 8:29,30; Eph. 1:4,11) Those that are still unconverted have nothing to do with this election: for them there is the offer of grace

and the summons to surrender. Outside, over the door of the
Father, stands the superscription: Him that cometh unto Me, I will
in no wise cast out.' This every one can see and understand. No
sooner are they inside the door than they see and understand the
other superscription: All that the Father giveth Me shall come to
me.' (John 6:37) Then they can discern how all things are of God:
first obedience to the command of God, then insight into the
counsel of God.

But then it is of great moment to hold fast this truth: He has
begun the good work. Then shall every thought of God strengthen
the confidence that He will also perfect it. His faithfulness, His
love, His power, are all pledged that He will perfect the good work
that He began. Pray, read how God has taken more than one oath
regarding His unchangeable faithfulness: your soul will rest in this
and find courage. (Gen. 28:15; Ps. 89:29,34,35,36; Isa. 54:9,10;
Jer. 33:25,26)

And how shall He finish His work? What has its origin from
Him is sustained by Him, and shall one day be brought to Him and
His glory. There is nothing in your life, temporal or spiritual, for
which the Father will not care, because it has influence upon you
for eternity. (Matt. 6:25,34; 1 Pet. 5:7) There is no moment of day
or night in which the silent growth of your soul is not to go
forward: the Father will take care of this, if you believe. There is no
part of your destiny as a child of God, perhaps in things of which
you have as yet not the least thought, but the Father will continue
and complete His work in it. (Isa. 27:2,3; 51:12,13) Yet upon one
condition. You must trust Him for this. You must in faith suffer
Him to work. You must trustfully say: The Lord will perfect that
which concerneth me. You must trustfully pray: I will cry unto
God that performeth all things for me. Christian, pray, let your
soul become full of the thought: The whole care, for the
continuation and the perfecting of God's work in me, is in His
hands. (Heb. 10:35; 13:5,6,20,21; 1 Pet 5:10)

And how glorious shall the perfecting not be. In our spiritual life, God is prepared to exhibit His power in making us partakers of His holiness and the image of His Son. He will make us fit, and set us in a condition for all the blessed work in His kingdom that He would have from us. Our body He will make like to the glorious body of His Son. We may wait for the coming of the Son Himself from heaven to take His own to Him. He will unite us in one body with all His chosen, and will receive and make us dwell for ever in His glory. O how can we think that God will not perfect His work? He will surely do it, He will gloriously do it, for every one that trusts Him for it.

Child of God, pray, say in deep assurance of faith: The Lord will perfect that which concerneth me. In every need say continually with great boldness: I will call on God, that performeth all things for me. And let the song of your life be the joyful doxology: From Him, and through Him and to Him are all things: to Him be the glory for ever. Amen.

Lord God, who shalt perfect that which concerneth me, teach me toknow Thee and to trust Thee. And let every thought of the new lifego hand in hand with the joyful assurance: He who began a work in mewill perfect it. Amen.

1. He that endureth to the end, the same shall be saved.' It brings but little profit to begin well; we must hold the beginning of our hope firm unto the end. (Matt. 10:27; 24:13; Heb. 3:14,16; 11:12)

2. The perseverance of the saints—in holiness—is one of the characteristic articles of doctrine of the Reformed Church. The grace of regeneration is inadmissible.

3. How do we explain the falling away of some believers? They were only temporary believers: they were partakers only of the workings of the Spirit. (Heb. 6:4)

4. How do I know whether I am partaker of the true new birth? As many as are led by the Spirit of God, they are the sons of God'

(Rom. 8:14). The faith that God has received me is matured, is confirmed, by works, by a walk under the leading of the Spirit.5. How can any one know for certain that he will persevere unto the end? By faith in God the Perfecter. We may take the Almighty God as our keeper. He that gives himself in sincerity to Him, and trusts wholly in Him to perfect His work, obtains a divine certitude that the Lord has Him, and will hold him fast unto the end.

Child of God, live in fellowship with your Father: live the life of faith in your Jesus with an undivided heart, and all fear of falling away shall be taken away from you. The living sealing of the Holy Spirit shall be your assurance of perseverance unto the end.

8816097R00127

Printed in Great Britain
by Amazon.co.uk, Ltd.,
Marston Gate.